TURNING· POINTS

How the Heart of Your Business is Formed in the Toughest of Times

JASE SOUDER

Published by
Hybrid Global Publishing
301 E 57th Street
4th Floor
New York, NY 10022

Souder, Jase
Turning Points: How the Heart of Your Business is Formed in the Toughest of Times
    LCCN: 2020925596
    ISBN: 978-1-951943-52-3
    eBook: 978-1-951943-53-0

Cover design by: Joe Potter
Interior design by: Suba Murugan
Copyediting by: Clauda Volkman
Author photo by: Nikki Incandela

https://worldclassspeakeracademy.com/

CONTENTS

FOREWORD

Jose Souder

Never trust a person who hasn't been broken.

Have you ever been (or are you currently) in a time of life that was so bad, you didn't know if it would ever end, how you'd get through it, or whether there would ever be light at the end of the tunnel?

Well, I have good news for you.

While times like these are horrible, you may or may not be aware of it yet, but you've been given a huge gift. It has two parts:

1. It's shaping you for massive success.

2. You're about to be in a position to make a difference in the world.

The hard times in life are the moments that destroy us—or they make us. The tough times refine us; they wake us up to a new life and new possibilities beyond what's known by the masses. Tough times force us to give up old ways and take responsibility for ourselves and our future.

I once heard a quote that went something like this: Most of the world lives life like they're having a fitful dream; they toss and turn, but they stay asleep—but those of us who are having a nightmare wake ourselves up.

It's the tough times that drive people to grow personally, find a new way, or champion a cause. The lessons you learn in the tough times are the lessons that will empower you the rest of your life. Your life will be better, forever, because of the times you're going through. So will the lives of the people you touch.

You aren't pulled through those times just for yourself—you're meant to pass it on. If you let yourself, you and your story will be used by God to help someone else. The lessons you've learned are meant to be shared with someone who needs help, right now, with that same thing. Your specific pain can help someone with that specific pain.

For example, if I, a single man, attempt to reassure a female client who's had a miscarriage, telling her it will all be all right, she'll probably say (or at least think), "Yeah, buddy, what do you know?"

On the other hand, one of my clients, who lost twins in the third trimester of her pregnancy, found a way to triumph through her pain. When she says, "There's fun after that," it's authentic and speaks the truth to others in pain. My client can talk to a woman who's had a miscarriage from a place of understanding the pain and offer hope, life and inspiration in a way that no one else can.

And no matter what "that" is for you, from your own place of triumph, you too will be able to touch lives in a way that no one else can.

And so do the authors you're about to meet. The stories in this book are all about "turning points"—the moments in life where we triumph over challenges.

From a teen out to change the world to entrepreneurs who change businesses, lives, and families, you're about to meet a group of people who are willing to share their tough times, and lessons, in hopes of inspiring you.

You'll find courage, faith, and hope in these pages. If you're struggling, I hope you find your turning point.

If you've been through that tough time, I hope you'll share it.

Lorena Arnold

Lorena Arnold is known for helping people achieve their authentic desires and life's work. She has a bachelor's degree in Computer Science and Information Systems from University of Phoenix, and she is now a Certified Money Breakthrough Business Coach. Interested in Lorena speaking to your group or association? Visit her website and sign up for her free newsletter.

www.lorenaarnold.com

THE GIFT THAT CHANGED IT ALL

Lorena Arnold

Have you ever wondered just how great and deeply fulfilled you could be if only you had the inspiration, strategies, and support to live up to your life's highest calling?

I went from being a struggling mom with no money, working two jobs, and raising my two sons to having cashflow properties and a $2M network in less than five years—but it wasn't always this way. Would you like to know how I did it?

Imagine if you could improve your financial condition, move out of lack and limitation, overcome obstacles, and become magnetic to abundance. Creating abundance is about much more than creating money in your life.

In this chapter, I'm going to share with you my pivotal story—the story that changed the course of my life and allowed me to find the freedom and flexibility to pursue my true calling.

Financial Independence is not about drinking cocktails on a beach for the rest of your life. It's about spending your precious years on earth doing something other than sitting behind a desk, counting the minutes to 5:00 p.m. and wishing you were somewhere else.

I am not here as a real estate investor to tell you how to use your money, nor I am a financial planner to tell you where to put your money. My mission is to share with you WHY and HOW you can have a new conversation with money—a conversation that can guide you to mastering your mindset about money and financial freedom.

I believe a woman should not be dependent on a spouse (partner), corporate America, social security, or a pension.
I believe financial stability gets rid of shame, helplessness, and guilt.
I believe in abundance, not scarcity.
I believe that life is too short to take the slow route to wealth.

My Story

There I was, on my first blind date after a devastating divorce that ended my eighteen-year marriage. My friends from the divorce group had set me up with this very handsome guy. He was a Realtor by profession and a very dedicated Tony Robbins follower. He asked me in—a very blunt way—several questions many people need to ask themselves:

- What do you really want?

- What is next for your life?

- What are your priorities?

Tears started following down my cheeks. "I don't know," I responded. I just knew deep inside my heart that something had to change. I could not continue living with two jobs, no goals, no vision, and nothing to strive for.

Like many women, I had grown up with the belief that if I held on to a marriage, everything would be OK. Yet I was drowning in despair, drowning in bills, and my only way out was to literally stop the world and get a divorce.

I cried in that restaurant like a lost little girl; I needed to find my path again.

Needless to say, it was not the greatest impression for a first blind date. But a couple of days later, he left a book on my doorstep—a gift that would dramatically change my life—and I never saw him again. People come into your life for a reason, a season, and a lifetime, and I believe he came into mine for a reason: to give me hope. The book was *Rich Woman* by Kim Kiyosaki, and it taught me to have courage and confidence and take inspired action so I would never lose sleep over money again. It taught me to take control of my financial future, stop looking for some rich Prince Charming, and achieve true financial independence. This was the first of many other books I read and seminars I attended about money, independence, and entrepreneurship. That gift changed it all.

I made a decision for my life; I made a promise before God and the universe that I would never again be poor again.

The first step I took was my personal development. There are only three ways to create wealth and abundance: 1) start your own business, 2) invest in real estate, or 3) invest in the stock market. I dove into real estate, learning all I could about buying and holding and growing a rental portfolio. I followed the stepping-stones for the wealth formula of 3 -2 -1: wholesale three, buy one flip; flip two and buy a rental property; do that five times and voila! My portfolio grew, and so did my net worth. The next step I took was to start a personal coaching business to teach other women the stepping-stones for wealth and help them learn to create, invest, and manifest money. I realized that a lot of women (and men) need a better understanding of the flow of money and time. I started providing value by sharing my contributions and knowledge with the purpose of sharing the wealth and abundance. The most transformational work is to help other women find their life's work—so they get paid what they are worth and create a new money story with fast-track success and unstoppable confidence. I love coaching women entrepreneurs, using a proven framework, strategy, and intuition.

Lessons Learned
As I began to study money, business, and entrepreneurship in the school of life, I learned the most important concept for creating all the wealth I would ever need: women have more money—and power—than ever before.

Then I asked myself, "If women have more money and power than ever before, why are they still so conflicted and unsure of how to deal with it?" Even women who are making more money than ever are still not comfortable with or confident about their money.

Lesson #1: The answer came in the form of another question: "What do you want from your money?"

So I asked myself, "What do I really want?" I wanted independence. Choices. The knowledge that money will last as long—if not longer—than I will. And, oh yes, less stress—much less stress. I found that most women don't openly discuss their income, net worth, and level of debt.

Lesson #2: I learned to conquer my fears so I would never have to look back and say that I regretted not pursuing what might have made me happy.

I am a firm believer that you cannot allow past negative experiences to cripple you or prevent future happiness. It is a natural human emotion to protect yourself against pain. But playing it safe keeps you stuck in a place you don't want to be. Then you look up one day and realize your life has passed you by, and you never got to do what you really wanted to do.

Lesson #3: Before I could attract the abundance I really wanted, I had to shift my perception of myself and my beliefs about deserving to have it.

Lesson #4: Time stops for no one. You can have all the money in the world, and if you lose the money, you can get it back. But you can never get back time. Once it's gone, it's gone. Our lives are precious, and how we spend our time is critical. Nobody else is responsible for our happiness.

I am not a financial planner or an accountant or a CPA. I understand the spiritual laws of money along with the human-made laws of money. Financial independence means freedom. *You* can achieve financial independence.

Yes, *you*. I know your story because I've lived it. Yes! I journeyed through tough times and many painful situations. I hit rock bottom! There is an infinite moment when you know you can fix it. You realize you got this. Your happiness is not up to anyone else to provide . . . it is up to YOU. Be true, be strong, and be aware of your happiness—because not everyone has a Prince Charming.

And besides, once you realize the fact that no one is going to be responsible for you, it's an awesome feeling! It means that personal joy and happiness can be created with courage and confidence-inspired action. You are suddenly in complete control of your own destiny.

A woman's financial independence is complete freedom; it's dependence on your own self. How amazing is that? You have the luxury of paying for your own happiness without depending on a spouse, a partner, corporate America, social security, or a pension. I know you can do this—because I did. I'm passionate about transforming women's lives emotionally, professionally, spiritually, and financially. Using these Four Quadrants for an Abundant Life, you too can achieve financial independence.

Erin Athene

Erin Athene is the co-founder of Mint CRO. Erin co-founded a $20 million software company and has advised hundreds of startups. She now trains entrepreneurs and marketers on an engineering approach to marketing that delivers 2X to 10X repeatable growth. Erin lives with her family in Kelowna, British Columbia.

www.mintcro.com

ENGINEERING MIRACLES

Erin Athene

One November evening in 1998, my roommate came home from work and said to me with hushed excitement, "I just made $250,000!"

We were best friends from college, in our mid-twenties, working entry-level jobs in Seattle—she at an online bookstore, and me at a clothing store. We both made about $9 an hour.

But when she started her job just one year before, she had received a small amount of company stock options as part of her compensation.

She hadn't thought much about it at the time, but as the share price continued to increase, and the stock kept splitting, she went from living paycheck-to-paycheck to owning a quarter of a million dollars almost overnight.

I was incredibly inspired. I thought, *Wow—if she can achieve this amazing wealth as a young woman—and we're not so different!—why can't I?*

This question awakened an insatiable curiosity to discover how wealth is created—and unleashed a bulldog-drive inside me to do it—both of which were completely new sensations I'd never felt before.

Eyes opened, I went in search of my own *Big Dog* opportunity: a high-growth company I could build with my sweat equity, and own a part of, so that I could fund my life dreams, too.

By the way, that little online bookstore my roommate worked at?

It was called Amazon.com.

"When the Student Is Ready . . ."

I had crossed paths with an elderly gentleman named Gary at a local health club. After a few years of bumping into him each week, I finally asked him what he did for a living. I was shocked to learn that all this time I had been chit-chatting with the managing director of the oldest angel investment group in Seattle, which he co-founded along with Silicon Valley Bank.

Intrigued, I asked him if I could ever be a "fly on the wall" at one of his meetings and listen to what investors knew about selecting high-growth companies.

He agreed, and this began four years of one of the most valuable mentorships of my life.

Gary would call me on a Thursday and say, "I'm a panel judge for a startup competition next week and have 40 business plans to review this weekend. What are you doing?"

I would drop everything and show up at his office early Saturday morning. Gary would stack a huge pile of business plans on the desk next to me with a thud, and we would go through them for hours, each reading and rating them in silence, and then debrief.

Eventually I got more involved in screening deals for his angel investment group. Volunteering at those meetings provided me with exclusive access to the candid debriefs between investors, and rare insight into exactly what they looked for in private equity investments. I learned about the opportunities, problems, and solutions from the company's perspective, along with the risks and gaps that savvy investors saw.

I began to recognize patterns.

Then one auspicious day, I met my first business partner. He was a former Microsoft techie and fit some of the "industry expert" patterns I had learned to recognize. He wanted help launching his enterprise software solution and asked me to review his business plan.

The plan was a geek-speak disaster, but thanks to the years of mentorship from several VCs and angel investors, I felt confident I could contribute. I had a clear vision for the framework and business fundamentals required to build a company with a good shot at success. So we formed a partnership and launched our new company, Topaz Bridge, out of his living room.

My Bridge to Purpose

We went all in, built an incredible team, had savvy investors backing our venture, and after 17 months, we miraculously landed a Fortune 500 client and closed our first investment round.

Suddenly our little startup was worth $20 million, and as one of the co-founders, I owned a big chunk of that equity.

I thought, *This is it! This could be my very own Big Dog.*

But six months later, we were out of business. We weren't able to survive the recession that was still crushing the economy in 2009.

I was heartbroken. Grieving the loss of my failed startup, I moved to Victoria, the small-town capital of British Columbia, Canada, for a slower pace and a chance to heal.

To my surprise, I discovered that Victoria had a $4 billion thriving tech community. Soon I was invited to be an Advisor/Executive-in-Residence at the local tech accelerator, VIATEC.

I owed it to my mentors to share the knowledge they had generously poured into me. So despite having a $20 million failure as my credentials, I accepted the role, and eventually trained and advised hundreds of early-stage tech companies on the Lean Startup Method and Market Validation.

To test my growth skills, I simultaneously volunteered to launch the local Victoria chapter of Ladies Learning Code as its Chapter Lead. I treated this little non-profit chapter the same as I would have advised a fledgling startup. We validated the market, recruited a core team of rock star volunteers, and created demand to launch with sold-out workshops. The approach was an overwhelming success: we became the fastest growing chapter in Canada. Within a few years, we taught thousands of women and children beginner coding skills, empowering them in digital literacy. It was beyond rewarding, and I found purpose helping to transform lives and open doors for more women to succeed in the male-dominated tech industry.

Another mentor of mine, Dr. Yvonne Coady, a PhD in Computer Science and professor at the University of Victoria, approached me with the idea of building a diverse team of at least 50% women developers to build gender-inclusive websites, software, and digital marketing campaigns. So in 2016, we launched my second tech company: Purpose Five Ventures.

After earning $250K+ our first year, we were firmly on the road to success, and we worked with Ernst & Young and the Province of B.C. to build a master database for the government in our second year.

But behind the scenes, I lived in the high-stress, "feast-or-famine" roller coaster that is so common to agencies: we either had too many clients all at once, or not enough, and our business reeled from the unpredictable dips in revenue.

Worse, my growing concern was the underlying business model of digital agencies: clients hired us to build high-quality, beautiful websites and campaigns, but what they really needed was qualified leads, sales, and reliable, engineered business growth. Without these issues solved, they would continue to struggle.

This dirty secret of the web design and marketing industry kept me up at night. Even the best-intentioned digital experts relied on guesswork. Real-time data from market feedback was usually absent from key decisions.

Basically, these "experts" didn't know how to reliably grow companies.

It all felt wrong to me based on my experiences evaluating and growing startups, but I was stuck in an unprofitable agency hamster wheel and didn't know of an alternative.

That is ... until I met Jessica Jobes, my future business partner. She had spent eight years on a top engineering team at Microsoft. Her team of 3,000 engineers running 230,000 tests per month had cracked the code on hyper-growth. Together they had achieved consistent user acquisition growth month after month—*for forty-nine months straight*. She took that remarkable experience and set out on her own, developing a simple yet brilliant engineering approach to marketing.

As an experiment, my team tested this methodology on one of our clients: in three weeks we **DOUBLED** their conversion rate while reducing their ad costs.

Then Jess and I recruited a group of beta clients to test how quickly we could train a diverse group of business owners to engineer consistent growth results, and to our delight, they produced off-the-charts results:

- One business owner tripled her website conversion rate from 7% to 21% in a week.

- One client immediately saved thousands in ad spend.

- One company doubled its monthly revenue in 30 days.

This was a line in the sand.

I knew from that point forward I would never go back to guessing about marketing, ad campaigns, or arguing about web design preferences, knowing this wasn't the key to real business growth.

My entire body relaxed. I could finally help business owners solve their true growth challenges.

Jess and I co-founded our new company in 2019, Mint CRO (Conversion Rate Optimization).

We "ate our own dog food," as they say at Microsoft, meaning we used the same methodology we sold to other companies to grow our startup from . . . *zero to $1 million in sales in our first year.*

Eight months later we made our second million . . . *during* the market disruption caused by the COVID-19 pandemic.

Our "overnight success" was two decades in the making, but finally my third tech company ticks all the boxes:

- High-growth business . . . ✓
- Equity ownership . . . ✓
- Purpose-driven . . . ✓

And the best part?

We get to pay it forward: Mint CRO gives thousands of dollars in scholarships to entrepreneurs and women-owned companies that want to accelerate their business growth.

It's amazing how powerful this simple method—using an engineering approach to marketing—can fuel real business growth.

Every day, company after company, we get to see the astonishment and joy on our clients' faces when they finally achieve hyper-growth results from learning to *engineer their own miracles.*

We have the privilege of empowering business owners to grow like the Big Dogs—and I am proud and deeply grateful to be a part of it.

Dr. Lori Beth Bisbey

Dr. Lori Beth Bisbey is a psychologist, sex and intimacy coach, author, podcast host, and speaker who has been helping people for more than thirty years to create and maintain meaningful relationships with sizzling sex (and without shame). Dr. Bisbey hosts *The A to Z of Sex*® podcast.

www.drloribethbisbey.com

FROM VICTIM TO SURVIVOR AND BEYOND

Dr. Lori Beth Bisbey

When I was nine years old, I made myself a bottle to live in as I waited for my Master—like Jeannie on *I Dream of Jeannie*. I already knew what turned me on sexually. That isn't strange—most people have an idea of their sexuality by then; we just don't usually identify that this is the case unless we are not heterosexual. I understood that my desires were different from the desires my friends had.

In high school when we were all dating, I really understood how different my desires were. I wanted to be overpowered, to surrender. I had shame around my desires, but I didn't know what to do about that.

I grew up in a household where gaslighting was the norm and boundaries were rarely observed. Both my parents would walk into my bedroom without knocking and without my permission. I didn't feel comfortable with someone walking in when I was undressed, so I asked for a lock on my bedroom door. My mom told me "not to be ridiculous." These boundary violations made me feel like my body did not belong to me.

The gaslighting I experienced was worse. I was often told that I was making things up when I told a story about something that happened to me. One of my uncles was always overly familiar. He would make sexually suggestive comments. When I complained about this, I was told that I was misinterpreting his intentions.

23

Gaslighting teaches you not to trust your own instincts and feelings. When you cannot trust your own gut feelings, it places you at risk for all types of abuse.

Gaslighting makes you feel crazy, and the only way to stop feeling so off balance is to adopt the views of the person doing the gaslighting and try to take control wherever you can. When people run over your boundaries, the only way to keep yourself emotionally (and often physically) safe is to become a control freak, and that is what I did. I learned very young that being in control was a way to limit the amount of pain (both emotional and physical) I experienced in life.

Being in control can be a positive thing in many areas of life. But being aggressively in control makes sex and relationships extremely difficult. In order to experience orgasm, you have to be able to give in to the sensations. To do this, you have to be able to trust your partner and to let go of control.

When I was nineteen, my best friend introduced me to Damien. He was older, handsome, and exciting—and he was excited by the same things sexually that excited me. Our desires fit together perfectly. He swept me off my feet. I quickly agreed to follow his lead, and before I knew it, I had agreed to surrender to him. I thought he was The One.

When we were first together, it was perfect; he didn't push me past any limits. He was patient and caring. Then one day he turned into a monster. He held me captive for five days, and during that time, he beat me and raped me repeatedly. He choked me until I died. Literally. I came back to life with him pounding on my chest and giving me mouth-to-mouth resuscitation.

My whole life changed as a result of that experience. I was devastated, and I developed post-traumatic stress disorder (PTSD).

I had nightmares every night. I had extreme anxiety, I startled easily, I trusted no one. I was frightened and tense all the time because I was petrified that he would find me again. At night before going to sleep, I would pace my small flat, walking the perimeter over and over. I checked all the windows and doors multiple times before I could get into bed.

Every time I had sex, I had a flashback. He was there. The flashbacks felt so real that it was as though my partner was Damien. I was no longer in the present.

I started therapy weeks after being held captive by Damien, and while the therapy kept me stable, I still had symptoms of PTSD.

I suffered in other ways too; I felt tremendous shame about my desires, even more shame in light of what happened, and my relationships suffered. Because I could not accept my desires or myself, my relationship choices were abysmal. I chose people who were emotionally unavailable, had substance abuse issues, and also had PTSD.

These relationships didn't work; they only left me feeling worse and like I needed to hold even tighter to control. I became even more of a control freak until I controlled myself into a corner. I couldn't relax. I couldn't allow someone else to take control of even something like cooking a meal.

When I went to university, I studied broadcast journalism. I love to write and to be on stage. I wanted to use both my writing skills and my love of entertaining, and television journalism seemed the best way to do this. After Damien, though, it didn't make sense anymore.

All I wanted was to figure out how to stop being traumatized and then be able to help other people recover from trauma. I switched to studying psychology and set out to become a clinical psychologist. In graduate school I discovered a trauma therapy specifically used to treat PTSD that was completely different from the therapy I had experienced, and it was amazing.

After being at the mercy of the PTSD for eight long years, I decided to try this new therapy—and after only a five-day intensive, it was all gone. No more flashbacks. No more intrusive thoughts. No more fear. No more symptoms of PTSD or depression. I still had work to do on myself, but for the first time in eight years, I no longer worried about Damien. I no longer felt like a victim—or even like a survivor, whose life is identified by a traumatic experience.

I had my life back. I finished my master's degree, the coursework for my PhD, and my internship, and then I met my first husband at a conference. He was British. We got engaged, and I moved to England to marry him.

In England, I did my dissertation research for my PhD, comparing treatments for crime victims with PTSD. I set out to scientifically prove that the treatment I experienced works.

I set up my practice and began working with clients, using the incredible method that helped me. I spent my work time helping other trauma survivors leave the trauma in the past and regain their lives.

I spoke in front of audiences about moving from victim to survivor and beyond. I taught therapists how to use this therapy. I co-authored a book in 1998 on PTSD that focused on this treatment method.

My life was fantastic, with one exception: my relationships. I couldn't trust fully in a relationship, and this impacted my marriage. I couldn't trust own gut instincts, so I dismissed my concerns about my husband's drinking and married him anyway. I couldn't surrender, so pleasure was extremely difficult. After eight years, my husband and I divorced.

I looked for a way to deal with the shame that still remained around my desires and my inability to give up control. As a therapist, I was actively working with couples and individuals on sex and relationships. Many of the women I worked with had experienced sexual violence and also had difficulty with their sexual relationships. I started trying a variety of therapy, coaching, and spiritual practice methods in an effort to get rid of the persistent shame I felt. Eventually, a combination of experiential and reflective practices worked.

First, I focused on getting rid of shame and relearning to trust my gut instincts. I learned to set boundaries and feel comfortable doing so. I learned to evaluate risk when choosing partners.

Next, I worked on surrender. I learned to differentiate between things that were healthy to control (my own reactions, my behavior, how I responded to any situation) and things I could not control (anything else—particularly other people and the outcome of any given situation). I learned that surrender gave me the means to be in the present, while controlling everything took an immense amount of energy and distracted me from all possibilities, all potential lessons and also all potential joys. I worked on surrendering to my higher self/power/ understanding of the Divine, and I trusted that by giving up control I would reap rewards and move along the path designed for me.

I worked on surrendering control to a partner, allowing them to lead, which allowed me to learn the joy of just accepting and experiencing during lovemaking.

The most important lesson I learned through this process is that surrender is the key to me being in flow. When I am in flow, I am on purpose, and all things come easily to me. When I hold tight to control, things become difficult. For me, surrender is a spiritual concept that is now integrated into my relationships. I surrender to a power higher than myself, and I surrender to that part of myself that works in my best interests.

After integrating my experiences and finally becoming comfortable with my own sexual desires, I started working with my therapy and coaching clients to help them to experience the same results. Once my shame was gone, I began to shine. I finally had exciting and satisfying sexual relationships, and this made an incredible impact on my other relationships too.

I met my second husband in 2009, and we have been happily together ever since. Our relationship is the first one I have had with someone who sees and loves all of me and with whom I have never felt shame. Our relationship suits us both and allows us both to live fully and out loud. Surrender is an integral part of my relationship with my husband. I am finally in a relationship where all my needs are met.

I use my unique combination of talents to help my clients create and maintain meaningful relationships that have sizzling sex without shame. I help people who have experienced all sorts of trauma—from divorce to extreme violence—to move from victim to survivor and then beyond back into life. I teach emotional, social, and relationship skills that bring clients to their authentic expressions of self and through that to their most authentic relationships. I specialize in working with people who have gender, sex, and relationship diversities. I provide a judgment-free, shame-free space and the tools these clients need to create the relationship styles that bring them the most pleasure, joy, and love.

I returned to broadcasting by starting a podcast, *The A to Z of Sex*®, in 2016 and presenting regularly on stages of all sizes. The authentic energy I now feel allows me to reach more people through my writing, podcasting, and speaking. Speaking has allowed me to touch people directly in a larger group and give them tools to create change.

The more integrated you are, the more energy you bring to all that you do. If you are carrying shame about any part of yourself or your life, this is communicated through everything you do. People feel it as a point of disconnection and then find it hard to believe and/or relate to your message. When there is authenticity, there is no disconnect, and you bring your full energy and attention to everything. The power of your message is exponentially increased as a result. You shine, and people are drawn to your energy.

My present life is incredible. I wake up each day knowing I am where I need to be and doing what I need to do. I have a daily practice that helps me to stay on my path. I was reborn at nineteen, though I did not realize it at the time. Now at fifty-eight, I greet each day in the knowledge that I have been gifted this time and that surrender allows me to use time to the fullest.

Liz Bull

A certified coach, medical intuitive and master energy healer, **Liz Bull** helps busy professionals clear old trauma and hidden energy blocks so they can make more money, lose weight without dieting, and lead lives they love. She's the author of *Your Amazing Itty Bitty Diet FREE Weight Loss Book*.

www.lizbull.com

NINE WORDS THAT CHANGED MY LIFE

Liz Bull

As the manager of training and development for a big bank in Montreal, I had risen in the ranks and was proud of my accomplishments. I was the first woman in the bank's history to have the title of manager. I was the only woman at the Institute of Canadian Bankers. I was the envy of my friends. The money was great, and the benefits and perks were amazing. Yet there was a nagging discontent.

It got worse when I was sought after by an even larger bank to do manpower planning in their international division. As I sat in an interview with six SVPs in the boardroom overlooking the Saint Lawrence River, I felt every hair stand up on the back of my neck. Why? Because every day I went to work, I felt like I was losing another part of myself. I felt like a square peg in a round hole. I mostly felt like an alien . . . or an imposter. In that boardroom, I felt like I was about to enter a dark place from which I would never return—so I declined the offer.

I knew I needed to change, but I didn't know how.

I learned that if you know you need to move, and you don't, bad things happen.

The discontent persisted. It turned into chronic migraines, weight gain, and low-grade depression.

I lived for weekend art workshops and classes. That's when I was alive and happy. While I was having success in the banking industry, I have always been an artist. Ever since I was a child, my dream had been to study design at Parsons School of Design in New York and have a career in the arts as an architect. But, like many women of my generation, I had been told that girls don't do that. Instead of going for my dream of being an architect, I became an art teacher. I found that frustrating rather than satisfying, so I gave it up and moved into the corporate world, where at least the money and benefits were good.

So there I was . . . weekend art workshops made me feel alive and mitigated the soul-deadening workweek of my corporate job.

Jim Collins said, "Good is the enemy of great." I had it good, but I wanted great, which for me was in the arts. I was scared, frustrated, angry, worried—and stuck! I didn't know what to do because I was paid well and had great benefits. I thought to myself, *Maybe it IS crazy, ungrateful even, to want more.*

My turning point came one cold winter night as I was listening to a lecture at the Harvard Club. The topic was career planning, and the presenters talked about how people delay real life—meaning doing what they would really love to do—until they retire. A lot of heads were nodding in the room, including mine. I knew they were talking to me. That was exactly what I had been doing.

Then it came—the question that changed everything for me. The presenters asked, "What if you get run over by a bus?" I bolted upright in my seat. Chills ran down my spine. It was a real possibility that at any moment it could all be over. The lesson hit me, and I realized there is no guarantee. Those nine words changed my life.

I had been putting off real life. I had been living someone else's idea of what my life should be. I was postponing my dream for some grand plan that could evaporate in a heartbeat.

In that moment, I decided I was out of that corporate job—I would go for my dream.

Fear rose up and gripped my stomach. Doubts flooded my head. I had no idea how it was going to work out. *How in the world am I gonna do this? I have a mortgage. I have bills to pay. Maybe I'm too old to go back to school. Can I even get in?* I was uncertain. I was scared. *What if I failed?*

There was a part of me arguing for why I couldn't, arguing for why it wasn't a good time, why it wasn't convenient or easy. Another part of me knew that great opportunities never show up when it's convenient or comfortable. I was about to learn that great things occur on the other side of what's comfortable.

I decided to let the part of me that wanted my dream win over the part of me that was terrified.

Emotionally I changed, and I decided I would take the leap. My husband and I started talking about how we could make this change. I started looking at how I could get into art in a way that worked for me—making good money doing what I loved. I had no desire to be a starving artist!

We started looking to make a change, and I wish I could say that this happened immediately—that I just took the bull by the horns and quit my job the next day—but I didn't. I dragged my feet for a bit . . . and then I learned another big lesson: Once you decide, things start to happen.

Even though I hadn't left yet, things started to happen. The moment you decide, you change; there's a reorganization that happens in your brain and body that causes energetic changes in you . . . and in the Universe. Your change affects the energy of the Universe, and all sorts of things occur to support you—things you could never have imagined.

And so, the Universe took over.

Within months, the bank reorganized, and I was out of a job.

At first I was in shock. *I am out of a job,* I thought. *There goes my plan to wait until retirement. I have a mortgage. How will I manage this?*

Then I had another thought: The decision in me had triggered the Universe to conspire to help me, and it forced me out of that job I hated. I was free. Along with my freedom came a very nice severance package! The severance package was big enough that I didn't have to work for a while, and I could see about getting into school.

But that's not the biggest part. Remember how I had been thinking I'd wait to do art when I retired? Within a year the bank went out of business. There would have been no retirement!

So now the path was wide open for me, and I went for it.

The crazy thing is that when I went for it, even more things happened in my favor. Things that I thought should never have occurred happened! The application deadline for design school had passed, and yet, because I was going for it, I talked my way in and secured the last spot in the class. I finished first in my class that year.

Because I decided and was going for it, the Universe kept stepping in to help. That childhood dream of attending Parsons School of Design? Out of nowhere my husband got a job in New York, and I was able to transfer to Parsons. Once again, the deadline for admission had passed, and yet I still got in.

I found a way to be in the creative field, make the money I wanted, and be fulfilled. I became an award-winning lighting designer. I became senior vice president of the firm that's best known for lighting the Empire State Building and then formed my own lighting design company. My work has been on TV, in newspapers and magazines, and on the front cover of the prestigious *Architectural*

Record. I was truly happy and fulfilled and enjoyed a great career.

Eventually it was time to move to the next phase of life, and I became intrigued with energy work and healing. I discovered that I had a talent to help people heal, and I longed to share these newly discovered gifts.

This time, I did not wait! I decided and went for it.

I enrolled and went through rigorous training in a number of modalities, including full spectrum healing and hypnosis, and I became a certified Life Mastery consultant. I attended intensive and lengthy certification trainings.

I discovered that there's an elegant, reliable, repeatable system for how to turn your dream into reality, based on more than forty years of researching the most successful people on the planet. I applied this proven system to my life, and my life keeps getting richer and more fulfilling.

I am now living my dream as a medical intuitive, master healer, and life coach, a career that I love; I have deep, rich, meaningful relationships that I cherish; my health is better than ever; and I'm able to serve clients I love and help incredible people discover, design, and then live their dream life.

If you are in that space of longing and discontent in some area of your life, please don't wait to pursue your dream! Because . . . what if you get run over by a bus?

Janet Clason

Janet Clason and her husband, John, live in a suburb of Kansas City, where they are building their home inspection business to make it possible to live their best life serving others.

www.crownhomeinspections.com

BIG, BEAUTIFUL WORLD

Janet Clason

I enjoyed a great career in the corporate world working for the same company for twenty-three years. I loved developing teams and mentoring people. I enjoyed the creativity in solving problems every day. It was fun to be involved in constantly changing technology, and it was rewarding to work with so many different people.

The less-than-perfect side of this was the downsizing, layoffs, reorganization, and right sizing. This seemed to happen about once a year for seventeen years. As a manager, I was responsible for making decisions about who would keep their job and who would be cut. These decisions were difficult and heartbreaking.

While I appreciated the work and the people, the environment was toxic. We couldn't predict when another layoff was coming, so team members were usually uneasy. Some competition is good, but I don't think people collaborate well or take good risks when they are afraid of losing their jobs. They are too busy watching their own backs and avoiding conflict.

My husband, John, worked at the same company, and he volunteered to take a severance package early in this process. He took charge of his destiny and used the opportunity to start his own business. While working in corporate America, he was often stressed, grumpy, angry, and impatient. He was courageous to take this jump. It paid off immediately as his personality changed and he became excited about the future.

When John started his own business, he still had stress, but it was different. He seemed to be able to deal with it better because he was in charge, he knew that the work he was doing was for us, and he wasn't working to improve someone else's bottom line.

As my corporate career continued, I often considered volunteering for a severance package, but I didn't have a plan. It was scary to assume that I could replace my income before the severance money was gone. I considered joining John's company, but I was concerned about putting "all our eggs in the same basket."

So I stayed, despite the layoffs. I wanted to be part of the long-term solution, and I wanted to coach my team members in the midst of this difficult environment.

It has always been important to me to mentor and coach others. I believed that the company could be successful, and I felt I could help others with their transitions whether they were staying or leaving. It would seem like a betrayal if I decided to leave.

My position involved making decisions about reorganizing teams and laying people off, notifying those people of their job loss, and managing the remaining team members through the change. We would usually start the process weeks before the actual layoff, make decisions, keep those private while Human Resources reviewed, all leading up to the "notification day."

Then, one year, I wasn't asked to make those tough decisions.

I had recently started a new position with a new team and was excited about learning a new and growing part of the business. I didn't even realize "notification day" had arrived when my boss asked me to drop by her office. It was completely normal for her to call me into her office, and I was prepared to provide an update on my projects.

Instead, she said the words I had recited so many times: "Your position has been impacted ..."

What?

It took me a minute to digest what she said. Then all I could say was "OK." She finished the HR script that I had delivered so many times and asked if I had questions.

She is a strong and smart woman and a respected mentor of mine. I had seen how these situations were extremely personal to her in previous cycles of layoffs, and I knew the decision wasn't made lightly.

I could justify her decision because I had just stepped into a new role, so cutting me was the least disruptive thing to do. I also knew that the least disruptive decision would not have been made if I had performed better than the other team members. I felt like a failure. How would I tell my husband, family, and friends that I wasn't good enough to keep my job?

I knew we would be fine, but it was a horrible feeling. I wanted to do my part to maintain our lifestyle, so I started networking with everyone I knew, asking about their journeys and their careers, joining job seeker clubs, and applying for various different jobs to test my opportunities.

I attended training where my out-of-work peers would practice elevator pitches and interview skills. At these training sessions, I sensed so much negative pressure. People in my industry were all living on the edge of knowing they could be cut at any time. Many job seekers were bitter about not feeling valued. Many people in our city had been laid off from my same company and were resentful or sarcastic about it.

I cautioned my friends that these negative feelings were showing up in their interviews and could be a factor in not getting hired. However, I didn't feel "heard" because they said they would never actually say those things to a potential employer. I believe, however, that those underlying attitudes would still be felt by potential employers because I had conducted many of those same hiring interviews over the years.

I really didn't want to get back into a job or position like that. But what should I do?

I was thinking about my future when it hit me: I had been afraid to leave corporate America because it was familiar. It was scary to think about starting over and going into the unknown.

I started looking outside of my familiar circle and sought out different experiences.

I wanted all kinds of experiences to find out what was out there. I found networking meetings of small business owners. I even went to a bootcamp to learn about building websites and took advantage of opportunities to learn about digital marketing and other small business essentials.

The best part? These rooms were full of entrepreneurs. Instead of feelings of negativity and blame, the energy of the entrepreneurs was so different; it was positive and electric. These were people running their own businesses, with no guarantee of success, but they were in charge and took responsibility for their lives. They were curious, creative, eager to share ideas and learn about how others were finding success. I had to get to know them and learn what they loved doing and why.

I reflected back on my previous career, and once I was outside of that toxic environment, I could look back and see how bad it was. I believe I had become complacent with the known and afraid of the unknown.

From these entrepreneurs and trainings I learned to objectively evaluate my situation and be honest.

- Am I really in the position where I can do the most good in the world?
- How wonderful is my life really?
- What would make it better?
- How do I get there?

I realized there is a big, beautiful world outside of what I had known in corporate America. Going to work with my husband would not be a crutch or fallback position—it would be the perfect position.

While I hadn't left corporate America because I wanted security, I now realized that security comes from working for myself. The best position for me was to take 100 percent responsibility for my future.

Working for ourselves means there is no more fear of layoffs, no toxic environment, no one can fire us, and we can build what we want. We took on building this business to support our dreams, and also to support our employees, their families and their dreams. We're creating the lives we had dreamed about and one of the best parts for us, now we get to work together!

Also, I realized I was better equipped for success than I thought. I had attended coaching programs with my husband for years and used those ideas to build my corporate presence. Now I could really dive into those coaching programs, learn more about the business, and be a true help to him. We are thriving together and moving in the same direction, toward the same goals.

We wouldn't be here if not for people helping us along the way. People helped me change the way I thought and taught me to thrive in business. Loving people took an interest in me and showed me new experiences to expand my world. Now I believe it is also my responsibility to help others along this journey.

If you find yourself stuck but nervous about making a major change, I have a challenge for you.

Ask yourself the same questions I used, to evaluate your own situation:

- Are you really in the position where you can do the most good in the world?
- How wonderful is your life really?
- What would make it better?
- How do you get there?

Are you willing to pass it on? What about the people in your world? Do you know someone who could use a loving nudge to do the same evaluation? You could be the one to help them see beyond their current circumstances and take steps toward new opportunities.

Sarah Clarke

Sarah Clarke is a Women's Empowerment Coach. She helps purpose-driven women transform their relationship with food and body so that they can free up their energy and live a life of meaning.

www.sarahclarkecoach.com

WHEN THE GIRL IN THE MIRROR SAID "NO MORE"

Sarah Clarke

I can still remember the night I stood alone in my college bedroom, gazing into my reflection in the full-length mirror. It was quiet, and cold. A candle burned behind me on the dresser. My journal lay open on the carpet at my feet. Staring back at me was my twenty-year-old face, thoughtful, sad, and a little fierce. I had been here before and always backed off, but this time I was going to go through with it. I had come to a decision. Looking myself resolutely in the eye, I spoke the words quietly and clearly: "No more. I am never going on another diet again."

On the outside nothing changed. The same green eyes, the same short brown hair. On the inside I could feel the impact of my words. That they meant forever. For the rest of my life.

In that moment, I stepped over a threshold from all that came before, from my childhood into the unknown. I did not know if my life would get better once I stopped dieting, or what the future would be like. I just knew that it was time to put an end to my perpetual struggle with misery, self-rejection, and restriction.

It all began when I was in second grade, when to my surprise, my mom announced that I was going on a diet. Life seemed pretty normal until then. I loved to run around outside with my sister and friends, playing in the canal, catching tadpoles, riding my bike. I loved the beach, challenging myself to swim as far as I could. I was easily the fastest and best swimmer of all my friends. I could do a double barrel roll off the diving board. I was fearless and curious about the world around me, and I sought its wonder. I started reading early and loved books. Unlike so many kids I knew, I was an adventurous eater. Food was part of life's excitement to me—I loved trying new things. At that point in my life, my body was simply the vehicle I went around the world in. I had no judgment about it; I accepted it just as it was.

When my mom informed me that I would now be on a diet, she explained it meant I would have different food in my school lunch. Instead of sandwiches, I would eat Ryvita crackers with butter smeared on them, along with a container of yogurt. It was the early 1970s, and this was the epitome of "diet food," although nutritionally it probably was not that different than the beloved tuna sandwich I normally ate. Today, the irony is not lost on me that I thought it was all delicious. I took it in stride . . . until I went to school and opened my lunch box for the first time. The other kids noticed me eating the kind of food they had seen in TV commercials for "fat people," and that is when the teasing, name-calling, and bullying began.

I suddenly went from feeling like a normal kid to an outsider. My family had moved eleven times already, over three different continents, and I had become used to being the new kid from a foreign country. Learning to fit in was an essential survival skill, and I had become a natural at perfecting the rapid transition from one culture to another. I could blend in. All of a sudden, though, no matter where I was or what I did, I could not hide from the label of "fat kid."

My friends and family apparently believed it was their duty to tease, name-call, bully, and comment on my weight to correct my "moral failing." They said things like:

"You should like this; it's fattening."
"If only your belly was flatter."

"If you're hungry, that's a good thing—it means you're losing weight."
"You can't have that; it's fattening."

They called me "fatso," "fatty," and other names I have done my best to forget.

My body then became an uncontrollable thing that I had to be on guard against at all times. From that time on, into my teen years, I dieted, starved myself, and overexercised, all the time feeling that I was not OK as I was. I could not relax and be a kid; I couldn't just be myself.

I learned to turn the bullying on myself in order to motivate myself to get thinner. I did not know what else to do. I believed that if I could get thin, then I could be lovable again.

As I grew from a girl, to a teenager, and then into a young woman, I wanted to fit in. I longed to be attractive, which to me meant that I needed to be "thin." The confusion that arose and the fear of being rejected became woven into a constricted sense of myself as a female, and I found myself more and more subdued, sad, depressed, and confused.

Eating became too stressful, so when I ate, I checked out of my body. I also used food as a way to compensate for the loneliness and distress in my life. Because I was constantly trying to get the answer from outside of myself, I prioritized what the "experts" told me to do, I tried to eat in a way that pleased my mom, I listened to doctors instead of myself, I ate the way the diet books and magazines recommended, and I followed the movie stars' as well as my friends' diets. I suffered alone and without relief.

My turning point came in college, when I took body awareness classes that taught me how to meditate, work with the breath, and tune in to my body. I began to learn to inhabit my skin. The students held a weekly free-form dance that I found irresistible and delightful. This supported me in feeling beautiful exactly as I was. I felt that I had finally come home. Slowly, I discovered for myself the feelings of strength and agency as I grew into being a woman, and that is what brought me to that moment in front of the mirror.

"I am never going on another diet again." I still remember the exact words I said out loud, and now I realize I did not just make a promise to stop dieting; I also made a promise to stop striving for this impossible goal. To stop trying to embody the perfect woman. To stop seeking validation through others outside myself.

When I made that promise, there were no how-to books on emotional or intuitive eating, or how to recover after stopping dieting. I took a leap. I said no to conforming. I said yes to discovering my own path, and I succeeded.

Eventually I have come to understand that none of this was my fault—there was nothing wrong with me from the start. I didn't do anything wrong, and I was never broken. I was not the source of my wounding around my relationship with food and body. I have developed a sense of trust with my body, honoring that it is resilient, loyal, faithful, and in service to me. I no longer think it is out of control; in fact, it is its own creature and deserves to be treated well.

My relationship with food now belongs to me, and is defined by me, not anyone else. I choose what I eat, when I eat, and I'm able to enjoy food and determine what suits me best.

I love to move my body again. I have learned to listen better, to avoid hurting myself with overexercise; my body comes first, not my stubborn will. I no longer wait to buy clothes until I am a certain size and I get what I love and feel great in. I feel ease and confidence in simply being myself, which is the greatest gift I could receive as a result of this path I have been on.

Now my journey leads me to share what I have learned. I am excited to use the perspective and skills I have gained, and I passionately care about helping other women break out of the tyranny of self-rejection and body hate. It is my mission to empower women to find their own freedom and fall in love with their bodies and lives. Most of all I love watching my clients' faces as they make breakthroughs, find compassion for themselves, and become empowered to be their true and complete, unique selves. This journey continues to fascinate me as my own wounds heal into scars, and the impact of healing spreads to so many others.

Sheri Curran

Sheri Curran is a professional bookkeeper, author, and speaker. From her thirty-plus years of bookkeeping and entrepreneurial experience, she has developed the Curran Cashflow System. Sheri is a member of an elite group of bookkeepers across the US, a charter member of the Digital Bookkeepers Association, and an Advanced ProAdvisor with QuickBooks Online.

www.curranbookkeeping.com

I WOKE UP THIRTY YEARS LATER

Sheri Curran

That day will forever be etched in my mind. I was devastated. The feeling of dread and hopelessness overwhelmed me.

For more than thirty years, my husband and I had owned and operated multiple businesses. Entrepreneurship—we love being able to set our own hours and work as a family toward a common goal. It's so rewarding to be building and growing our own businesses and supporting others with employment.

My greatest contribution to our empire has been my expertise and training as a bookkeeper. Over the years I utilized and expanded my skills while I was raising our four boys. It was flexibility at its best. Those precious days with my sons are days that I treasured, made possible through entrepreneurship.

As the boys were nearing adulthood, I began dreaming for the next wonderful season of my life. I could do anything I wanted to do. So what would this next stage look like? What things did I wish I had more time to do? That was easy to answer: volunteering at our church and spending time one-on-one with those that needed encouragement in life, living near me or in poverty-stricken countries. I wanted more than being an encouraging friend; I wanted to bring others hope. This was my dream.

The day finally came. We had a nearly empty nest. I had thoroughly enjoyed my time with my sons, but they were now men who had their own dreams. Though we would always be a part of one another's lives, we would now be embarking on our own new journeys. It would be a new season for all of us. That was exciting!

One Saturday morning my husband and I sat on our couch to talk about life and our future goals. It was such a bright, happy day as we sat contemplating and strategizing. We were at a great place in our relationship and very happy with life. I was feeling so blessed. But as we were talking, I started to feel that something was off. Something felt different about our conversation this time. Then it happened. My husband hit me with a bombshell I hadn't expected.

He said, "Now that the boys no longer need you, you need to start contributing to our finances. I'm getting too old to carry the burden." I felt like my heart stopped. What did this mean? Was I going to have to look for a job? Not only had it been thirty years since I had been employed, but this would mean giving up my dream. Employment to me sounded like a life sentence. I was devastated. Depression and hopelessness flooded my emotions. My world came crashing down on me. That bright, happy moment turned into darkness and despair.

How had I not seen this coming? Had I known it all along, but just didn't want to recognize it? Regardless, here we were. We had worked for thirty years and had nothing to show for it. Other people our age had planned years in advance for their retirement years and were in a better position where they could enjoy a relaxing golden age. But for us, forget retirement.

We would have to work another thirty years instead.

The reality of where we were at this stage of life hit me hard. How did we get to this place? Why did we not pay attention to the signs along the way? What were we going to have to do to have a future?

I sat in desperation and tears for several hours. Trying to help, my husband offered multiple options: I could get a job, earn a degree in something new, start a new business. None of these were a part of my dream. After much agonizing, I came to the realization that my dream had died. I wouldn't be able to spend those multiple hours a day in the way that I had planned, encouraging, supporting, and serving others. I was going to have to earn a living. Apparently there was no way to make this scenario disappear, so it was critical for me to find the answers to two questions: What did we do wrong? And how could I still have a future and a dream with purpose and meaning?

Through more tears and more desperation, I began searching for the answers to my questions. First and foremost, I sought a way to move forward with hope for my future. Living a life of purpose and meaning was very important to me in addition to making a difference in people's lives. If I had to make a living, I needed to find a way to do it so I could still fulfill the desire in my heart to encourage, support, and serve others.

I considered my options. I was too much of an entrepreneur to consider employment. And there wasn't any other field I was interested in pursuing. I honestly really enjoyed bookkeeping, and I wondered if I could expand on what I was already doing for myself and my husband. I started realizing that, although bookkeeping came easy to me, it was an area of real struggle for other business owners. In fact, finding an expert bookkeeper was a rarity. As I studied and researched the possibilities, I began seeing how I could build a meaningful future and have an even bigger impact on people's lives than I originally had hoped for—by supporting other businesses in the area of their finances. I was beginning to dream again!

Now that I had a glimmer of hope for my future, I was ready to dig into the past and discover answers to what we had done, or not done, to put us in the situation we found ourselves in. I discovered we had missed out on some valuable insights and strategies that would have helped us prepare for future seasons and retirement. As entrepreneurs, we rarely looked at the numbers of our business. These numbers produced from financial reports are supposed to be the thermometer and indicator of the health and state of a business. So that should have been our first response. But it wasn't. Had we kept a close eye on this information, it would have shown us the need to save, cut back on expenses, and plan for the future of our business and our life.

We had the wrong mindset around money, causing us to spend instead of save. We made decisions for the moment, but we didn't consider the future. Decisions were made based on emotions or opportunities but not measured against the factual information that was just a click away. I now know that numbers are facts, and facts don't lie. When you have the right systems in place to track your finances, it gives you the facts. You need to know the facts to make the right decisions. This gives you confidence, which then helps you excel and achieve your dreams.

Having a plan is so important, but unfortunately we didn't have one. Like most entrepreneurs, we had times of feast and times of famine. Because of this, we never developed a rhythm for spending and saving. And unfortunately we never established a plan for how to handle the excess brought in during the times of abundance.

During the feasting years, we enjoyed the extra income and spent money on things we normally wouldn't have, just because we could. We enjoyed vacations and fun, expensive toys during those years. But we failed to use some of our extra money on preparation for the lean years as well as for our future.

Recognizing our mistakes was painful for us. We felt so much shame and regret, but knowing our numbers and having a plan for spending and saving was a huge step in making the necessary changes. After three short years of applying the healthy money habits we had learned, we were ready to prepare for our golden years. Shame and regret were turning to relief and hope for our future.

I was also now in a position to help other people discover their own money health and give them the tools they need to move their finances to a position of abundance and investing for their future. Every entrepreneur needs to know their numbers, understand how to read their financial reports, and plan for their future. It has become my passion to deliver these important truths and abilities to others' lives and businesses.

My new dream, my mission, is to help other people avoid the mistakes my husband and I made. I know the enormous impact healthy money habits can make in one's life. Understanding this firsthand brings me to a place of no judgment—just compassion and encouragement. I can actually now be thankful for the position we were in, because it gave me the opportunity to be a vehicle for change and hope.

I don't want anyone else to wake up after working thirty years only to find they now have to work another thirty!

Danny Forster

Danny Forster is a third-generation business owner, certified home inspector, and licensed real estate agent. Born and raised in southern California, Danny attended Cal State San Marcos before joining the family business. Outside of work, you can find Danny playing a round of golf, listening to a motivational podcast, or lending a helping hand in the community.

www.Forsterhomeinspections.com

THE CHOICE IS YOURS

Danny Forster

As a carefree sixteen-year-old, I had everything I could have imagined. I was young, full of life, not a worry in the world, and as I drove down to the local gym to play basketball with my friends, I had no idea my life would change forever.

I had been raised by a single mom. We grew closer with each passing year, and no matter what life threw at us, we always had each other. We shared laughs, tears, celebrations, and struggles. My mother never let me see how difficult it really was to be a single mom. She worked day and night to provide for me and give me a life some people only dream of.

Amidst all the joy and adventures, though, my mother struggled with addiction. She was an alcoholic, and I remember nights when she passed out and I was unable to wake her. In these moments, I turned to my grandparents; I could always count on them to come to my rescue. As I grew older, I learned to truly appreciate their support, and when life got tough and my mother couldn't be there for me, I knew I could always rely on my grandparents.

It wasn't until my early teenage years that I understood the severity of the situation. I distinctly remember feeling scared as my mother and grandparents argued in the other room. I couldn't hear the exact words, but I could tell something was wrong from the yelling and crying.

A few years later, my mother explained what had happened that night. My grandfather had finally threatened to take custody of me if she didn't get her life under control. In that moment, my mother claims she made the best decision of her life. She enrolled in a rehabilitation program and began her journey to sobriety. From this situation, I learned from my grandparents about doing the right thing, and again I turned to them for shelter and support.

If it wasn't for my grandparents, I don't know what would have happened to me or my mother. They showered me with love and gave me hope for the future. I'm sure it wasn't always easy, but they never let me down. They taught me that there will be times in life when you feel at rock bottom, and it's important to surround yourself with a support system to help you through those times.

Many years later, my mother was running a successful small business. She had completely turned her life around. Everything seemed to be going great . . . until that day when I was sixteen and returned from playing basketball. I found my mother lying on the bathroom floor, unresponsive. I didn't know what to do, so I called the two people I could always count on—my grandparents. It felt like an eternity waiting for the paramedics to arrive. My mother had suffered a heart attack and was no longer with us, and I was hopeless and heartbroken.

Once again, my grandparents came to my rescue. After my mother's passing, they brought me into their home. They continued to provide me with everything they could, and most of all, they provided me with love and support.

This was a dark time in my life. I was lost and miserable. I went through several stages of grief: sadness, anger, depression, apathy, and finally acceptance. During it all, I made poor decisions that could have led to lifelong consequences. Luckily, my grandfather continued to show up for me. Despite his own battles with grief, he was able to show me that life must go on and happiness is a choice.

Looking back, I realize how difficult it must have been for my grandparents. Parents are never supposed to bury their children. If I could go back in time and rewrite my story, I definitely wouldn't have picked these events. However, I am grateful for the opportunity to spend more time with my grandfather and learn valuable life lessons from him. Life is a gift, and you must cherish the time you have on this earth because tomorrow is never promised.

Fast-forward to my early twenties—I was now working alongside my grandfather, learning to run a multi-inspector home inspection business. Working with family is not easy. There were many tough discussions throughout the years about work ethic and leadership. In the beginning, I was naïve and thought being an "owner" meant I didn't have to work hard. After all, the business had been established for many years and had a strong reputation in the community. I couldn't have been more wrong.

My grandfather sat me down to face the harsh reality that he wouldn't be around forever. He was eighty-three at the time, and I was twenty-five. We talked about our business—and more importantly, our lives. This is when I really knew he loved and cared for me, and what came out of this discussion changed my life.

He flat-out told me he knew I was not a good partner in the business. He said that I was a good inspector/employee, but that there was a difference between working for a company and running a company. He told me he would die one day, and he said what he was doing was not for him.

Although it was tough to imagine a life without my grandfather, I knew it was inevitable. It was time for me to take business ownership seriously. I still wasn't sure what I wanted out of life, but I was certain I didn't want to let my grandfather down. I spent the next few years gaining as much knowledge and wisdom from him as I could. Our business and relationship drastically changed through this time. We watched the company grow in ways we didn't know were possible. Within the first year, we were able to increase our cash flow by over 25 percent and provide consistent paychecks to ourselves. This was a luxury we hadn't experienced up until this point.

It was a blessing to have my grandfather as a business partner, mentor, and friend. He instilled a strong work ethic in me and showed me how to be a better person. I watched him start every day with a smile and determination. He was never afraid to try something new or ask for help. He taught me that it's okay to be wrong, and he told me to never give up on my goals. Most of all, I learned patience. My grandfather always took the time to listen and talk with anyone. It was both a strength and a weakness. He was late on many occasions. However, the hearts he touched made it worth it. This is something I strive for every day. I try to take life day by day and not get caught up in the rushed pace of life. I never know whom I'll meet or how we might impact each other's lives.

Now my grandfather has passed, and I've taken over the business. I continue to use the life lessons he taught me to become a better leader and business owner. When it comes to interactions with clients and vendors, I treat everyone like family. I seek to be there for them when they're in need, I communicate clearly, I demonstrate the utmost integrity, and I go the extra mile to guarantee satisfaction. I am always looking for ways to improve and provide more value to our customers, whether that's from continued education, purchasing the latest technology and equipment, or giving back to the community.

I choose to live my life to the fullest each and every day. I know life can be taken from any of us without notice. I always do my best to listen to people, not be quick to judge someone for their actions, and give everyone the benefit of the doubt. I care for people and truly believe there is good in everyone. I understand that situations can change a person's behavior or attitude. Sadness or anger can spread quickly, but I believe happiness can spread just as quickly. Regardless of the situation, I always look for something positive to focus on and hopefully be a beacon of light in others' lives. I've learned that the power of doing something nice for someone, with nothing expected in return, can change not only you, but also the person you are interacting with.

I could have used my mother's death as an excuse to give up. However, my grandfather was not going to let that happen. It wasn't always easy, but it was worth it. I'm now running a successful home inspection company on my own. I've been able to help countless individuals and families find their forever home and know that it's safe and reliable. I've had the opportunity to touch lives in the community through donating my time and money whenever possible. I owe my success to my grandfather and have him to thank for where I am today.

Sonia Garcia

Sonia Garcia is a certified hypnotist and NLP practitioner specializing in the education and coaching of those who are ready to make a change in their lives. Her two decades of experience with transformational strategies aid her in supporting others in creating lasting change.

www.thechangequeen.com

HYPNOSIS—IT CHANGES LIVES

Sonia Garcia

As a junior in college, I was sailing along with a seemingly charmed life: good grades, great friends, living my passions. I was looking forward to the future I was creating for myself.

I had just returned to the U.S. from playing professional soccer in Guatemala. I was feeling uneasy, sick, and sleeping most of the day. I thought I had caught a bug. Turns out, I had caught a baby. I took a test and found out I was pregnant.

I was crushed. I had gotten pregnant near the end of a relationship, and the father was not going to be in the picture. Because of the beliefs I inherited from my family, I was full of shame and embarrassment. At that time, I didn't know I could be a single mom and still have a great life. I was devastated. It seemed that all my career aspirations were gone, and I thought my family would disown me for ruining my education.

Luckily my family did the opposite, and with their help, I completed my degree. I knew raising my son was my responsibility. While I had been hoping to be a mediator, now I was a single mom with a kid to raise on my own.

My inspirations were replaced with obligations.

I took whatever job I could get, landing a social work job. While it paid way less than I wanted, at least it allowed me to help others.

I quickly realized I would not be able to raise my son on that salary, so I returned to school to become a teacher. As a teacher, I worked my butt off at an inner-city school while taking courses to climb the salary table.

I quickly got burned out. Every day I would come home and head straight for the couch, with no energy to play with my young son. I no longer felt in control of my life; I was merely surviving.

I was experiencing massive self-criticism, shame, and guilt around my financial and personal condition—so much so that at one of my lowest points, I broke down crying in front of a classroom of teenagers.

I was doing the "right" things. I was working hard. Going to school. Trying to improve. Trying to make more money. Yet I found myself, even after all the hard work, broke and at a job where I wasn't valued.

I began to look elsewhere than the "go to college, get a good job" model for getting ahead. I was desperate for solutions. I invested in courses and coaches, and I committed to furthering my personal growth.

At one of those courses, a hypnotist invited us to attend his event. I remembered that I had come across hypnosis years before. It had really been an impactful experience for me.

My speech professor in college was a hypnotist. He would not repeat instructions or answer questions EVER! He said, "It is all recorded in your subconscious mind, and you should trust that you have the information you need."

This was jarring for a student like me. I relied heavily on my conscious mind, and it was uncomfortable for me to trust my own memories without clarifications. Yet the information he proposed seemed valuable. The professor also taught us that stress and anxiety block the flow of information from the subconscious mind, where all memory is stored like a video camera.

This knowledge really made a difference in my academic career. I would load my brain with information. When it came time to perform or take an exam, I relaxed into the activity so that my conscious and subconscious could work together. I became a very stress-free college student.

Before the course wrapped up, the professor showcased some more extravagant ways hypnosis can be used. It was mind-blowing to watch him use the power of self-hypnosis to snap a bear trap on his forearm without breaking the skin.

If that wasn't mind-blowing enough, the thing that made the biggest impression on me was when he chose a fellow student to participate in a hypnosis session in front of the class. I had thought this particular student was timid. The whole course he sat in the front, appearing insecure and requesting frequent direction and reassurance from the professor. This thirty-something-year-old man had a very childish demeanor.

The student confessed that he had problems with forgetfulness. The professor used hypnosis to take him back to a moment in his childhood when he had misplaced a book and his mother yelled at him. He was back in the moment and appeared to be traumatized by her response.

The hypnotist was able to help him resolve the emotions of that moment. In the student's mind, he found the book and had a loving interaction with his mother. When his awareness came back to the classroom, out of his relaxed-dream state, he was a new person!

His stance was confident, mature, and in control. His face seemed to change into that of a powerful grown man. He showed up completely different in what seemed an instantaneous manner.

I was in awe of the change. If my classmate could change instantaneously, anyone could—including me!

I felt a burst of energy flow through me; I was on a high I did not recognize. I remember crawling into my parents' bed that night. Sobbing with joy, I began experiencing overwhelming hope and gratitude for God, my parents, and the whole world. I was more excited about life than ever before.

In my heart and mind, with this powerful tool, I realized there was no past too horrid or wrong too great that could not be righted. I felt empowered with the knowledge that I could rewrite my story, thus making me a powerful creator that could redirect my future.

While I was so inspired by this brief exposure to hypnosis, I didn't have facility with it. When I got pregnant a couple years later, it didn't even enter my mind to seek out a hypnotist for help with my shame and guilt.

But now I had a new opportunity to use this amazing tool. I found myself in a position where I could rewrite my past to create a different trajectory. I knew I needed a change, and ideally the change would be as instantaneous as the one that man from my speech class experienced years ago.

I attended the first course and felt on fire with passion and a renewed sense of hope and energy. I broke through fears about approaching strangers, being uncomfortable, and taking action despite my ego and negative thoughts. Whatever fears or blocks I had before were gone! This allowed for new actions in my life, such as generating massive results in a short amount of time.

In less than a year, I had gotten an amazing new job, started the company of my dreams, and attracted the love of my life. I was powerful, confident, and free, equipped with the tools to make any change I desired.

I began to partner with my subconscious mind, the place where true change takes place. I found out that I can accomplish anything I set my mind on being, doing, and having. Thoughts, emotions, and patterns that are not serving me can be shifted to ones that are empowering, focused, and effective.

I was loving the changes in my life and was inspired to help others as much as I had been helped. The opportunity to get certified as a hypnotist presented itself, and I jumped in!

I was able to support loved ones immediately. My best friend's husband had passed away a few months before, and I knew in my heart hypnosis would support her with her grief, so we did a session together. Hypnosis supported her in finding peace and starting the process of true healing.

My clients were also getting amazing results!

One was able to gain clarity and redesign her marriage. After almost fifteen years of being on and off, they were able to fulfill their dream of having more children together. She attributes the shift to the hypnosis session.

Another client came to me because she was not getting adequate sleep. She had night terrors and required medication to sleep. After one hypnosis session, she reported that she had no more sleeping challenges and was experiencing a more renewed lifestyle.

I was over the moon to have these new skills to help others—and in such a powerful way!

More than anything, I feel passion, creativity, and power to instill change. I am able to see the qualities that make me uniquely me and how they are important in this world. Most of all I'm excited because I know this tool works for others, and I can support them in rewriting their past in order to have a new future.

Madison Hawley

Madison Hawley may only be a seventeen-year-old girl, but in her short time on this planet, she's lived life's great adventures and seen the darkest sides of drugs and alcohol. Through everything she's been through, Madison is destined to change the world.

I'M OUT TO CHANGE THE WORLD, ONE STEP AT A TIME

Madison Hawley

Before I tell you my story, here is what I believe:

I believe that feeling safe is a human right.
I believe kids don't choose their parents and shouldn't pay for their mistakes.
I believe that kids need someone to step up and help them when they can't help themselves.

I used to be a cheerleader. I've been to seventeen different states and eight countries. I'm in a speaker training program, and I'm going to change the world. But I wasn't always this way. I used to have no confidence in my abilities to help others, and I thought I had nothing to offer to the world—but now I know that's not true. Now I know that you and I can change the world, and here's where I want to start. Let me share about just one family I know, and how they represent so much of what is going on with kids today.

Feeling Safe Is a Human Right

In June 2020, my life changed. I was at my best friend's house. Her mom was upstairs, and her stepdad was downstairs. Her mom sent me downstairs to her bedroom to get something. I had been around them before when they were on drugs, but I was not prepared for what I was about to see.

When I opened the door, the first thing I saw were needles on the dresser. I saw her stepdad bent over . . . he was pulling his toes apart and shooting up heroin. Before I could even ask him for what I came down there for, my friend walked in, and so did her mom. They continued on with a normal conversation.

I left the room and went and cried on the couch in the living room. The only thing running through my mind was my dead cousin who overdosed a couple months earlier. I thought, *What if my friend ends up like him? What if her mom or I or someone else finds her hunched over on her nightstand . . . dead?*

My friend came into the living room and saw me crying. She asked me what was wrong, and when I didn't answer, it suddenly clicked and I knew what was causing me to cry: my sixteen-year-old friend wasn't even fazed watching her stepdad shoot up because she had probably seen it countless times. The worst part was that she found it normal.

How safe could she feel?

Kids Don't Choose Their Parents, and They Shouldn't Pay for Their Mistakes

Here are a couple examples of kids not choosing their parents.

My friend's mom and her stepdad had recently gotten clean. We thought everything was going great. Then one day we found her mom drinking and crying in her room. When we asked her what was wrong, she told us that they had both relapsed and she had been forced to call the cops on my friend's stepdad. When the cops arrived, he confronted them with a machete.

What kind of situation is that for a kid?

No kid would choose that.

No kid should pay that price.

Then her mom had me drive her to the liquor store so she could buy more alcohol. I didn't want to do it, but I felt like I couldn't say no to her. I couldn't say no to someone who was like a mom to me and who was crying and asking me for help. But I was worried that my friend would be mad at me for taking her mom to buy alcohol.

It's not fair for a trusted adult to put a kid in a situation like that. I was put in a bad situation and was paying the price for this adult.

My friend paid the price for her mom . . .

When I left my friend that night, her mom had a couple friends over—all nice people, and my friend's stepdad was gone. But not for long. . . . My friend knew something was wrong when she saw that her stepdad had come back.

She immediately went downstairs and saw her mom and all her drug friends doing meth.

Due to this, my friend stayed up all night to make sure her mom didn't do any harder drugs and overdose. Because of this, my friend wasn't able to go into work the next morning.

My friend paid the price for her mom again!

We were on our way to work to get our checks when my friend asked me, "How am I going to get my check?" I was confused and told her all she needed was her permit. That's when she told me that her mom had done meth off of her driver's permit, and now it was lost.

Her mom once told me she was her daughter's best friend for life, but can that be true when her daughter no longer has a driver's permit because her own mom did meth off it? Can that be true when she sees all the pain she has put her daughter and her five other children (none of which she has custody of) through and does nothing?

Kids Need Someone to Step Up and Help Them When They Can't Help Themselves

There are countless kids in similar positions as my friend—some even worse. The system doesn't always work; often there are ways around it, and that is why kids are left in these horrible situations.

Seeing what my friend's life was like, I felt as though I had no way to help her, that I was useless. I knew her being in that situation was wrong. I knew she shouldn't have to go through the things she went through, but I didn't know how to help change things.

It wasn't until I went to one of my speaker training events that things became clearer.

There I learned that the first step in helping, the first step in changing the world, the first step in changing anything, is bringing awareness to the situation. I realized I could do that.

While I was on the stage sharing my story, I looked into the audience and saw people crying; I saw that people were moved by what I shared. I received feedback that made me want to share this story even more. Then, when we asked the audience if they wanted to help my cause, if they wanted to do something or donate or help in some way, all the hands went up.

At that moment I realized I could be the start of a chain reaction to help kids.

I don't know what the answer looks like, and the problem is complex. It's not just about getting the kids out of their homes, because sometimes they end up going to a foster home that's not a great situation either, so that's not the solution. There are so many levels to all this . . .

But I do know that there *is* a solution, somehow, some way, for kids to feel safe, and for kids to stop paying for the mistakes of their parents.

I know for sure that kids need someone to step up and help them when they can't help themselves, and there are ways to accomplish that . . .

My family and our friends' family both opened our homes to my friend when she was going through a hard time. If you see a child suffering in their home, reach out—doing something is better than doing nothing.

I don't know how to solve this problem, but I'm trying, and I believe that if everyone started trying just a little bit, we could change the world. It's not that hard to reach out to a kid just to see if they're okay, and sometimes they don't have anybody else in their lives checking up on them.

I'm going to change the world one step at a time—and so can you!

Matt Hawley

Matt Hawley is the owner and general manager of Hawley Home Inspections LLC, which is one of the largest independently owned home inspection companies in the St. Louis metroarea.Matt has been inspecting homes since 2010, has multiple industry certifications,and is a highly qualified inspector trainer.

www.hawleyhomeinspectionsllc.com

WHAT'S KEEPING YOU FROM BEING THE BEST THAT YOU CAN BE?

Matt Hawley

The summer before starting kindergarten, I overheard my grandpa telling my grandma that my parents should not waste their time sending me to school because I was nowhere near smart enough.

His words planted a seed in my heart that I was not smart and did not matter.

His words rang in my ears, and on the first day of kindergarten, I did not feel like I belonged there. On day two, instead of going to class, I got off the bus at school and walked home by myself. I did that day after day for two weeks.

Only after *two weeks* did anyone notice that five-year-old me was not there, and this really made me feel like I did not matter. The seed Grandpa planted started to grow.

The next year I started at a new school where I was taller than all the other kids and soon became their target. I was picked on, made fun of, and told that I was fat and ugly. I even had a teacher tell me that I was dumb, worthless, and would never amount to anything.

The seed kept growing.

When I was thirteen years old, I tried alcohol for the first time, and for the first time in my life, I truly felt confident. Unfortunately, that did not last long, so eventually I drank more so I could feel confident again.

After high school I ended up working dead-end jobs. With no real future ahead of me, I decided to join the Army.

That summer, I got a phone call that a friend of mine had committed suicide. Later that night, while depressed and drinking, I told a girl I had a crush on about my friend committing suicide; her response was "If you miss him so much, maybe you should join him." The seed now grew into a full tree.

The very next night I attempted suicide—and failed, which made me feel like an even bigger loser; I couldn't even do that right.

After the Army, I took a job driving a truck. It didn't take me long to excel as a truck driver—it was easy for me to be gone for six to eight weeks at a time because in my mind, nobody cared whether I came home or not.

In 1995, I got married. The first year was great; we had a kid on the way, and I thought life could not get any better. Then one day my wife told me something was wrong with the pregnancy. In less than a week's time, she lost the baby, and my world collapsed. The voices telling me I was worthless became even louder, and I started drinking more than ever.

Before long she was pregnant again, and this time we were expecting twins. Unfortunately, we lost one of the twins, and my wife spent most of the pregnancy in the hospital on bed rest.

Even though she gave birth to a beautiful baby girl, my wife never got over the other two losses. She told me daily it was my fault that we lost the babies. Again, someone in my family was telling me I was not enough, and again I turned to alcohol.

By this point in time, that seed my grandpa planted had grown from a single tree into a forest of worthlessness and hopelessness.

My wife and I divorced, and I spent the next two years drinking hard and wishing I were dead. But every time I started down that path of suicide, I would see my daughter's face, and it would inspire me to keep pushing forward.

I met my second wife on a blind date, and after several months, *she* proposed to me! We got married the next year, and two years later we had a beautiful daughter together.

I had cut down on my drinking and thought I had it under control. What I did not realize was how much alcohol was actually controlling me.

In 2010 with the encouragement of my wife and family, I started Hawley Home Inspections. The first couple years were a struggle, and then finally everything took off. But as the business grew, my stress level skyrocketed. I began drinking more to control the stress.

On February 12, 2019, one of my business coaches, Mike Crow, asked me a question that would change my life forever: "What is keeping you from being the best that you can be?" At that exact moment I knew the answer to that question: drinking. The next morning, I got up and promised myself that for the first time in thirty-six years, I would not drink.

In the weeks that followed, Mike introduced me to two different world-renowned speakers that would change my life even more.

The first one was Thomas Blackwell. He taught me that when you speak with negative words, negative things in life will find you, and when you speak positive words, positive things will find you.

I realized that for years I had been repeating the negative words my grandpa spoke, and because of this, I had been bringing negative things to myself.

I learned to embrace the power of positive thoughts and positive words, and ever since I have been attracting life and positivity to myself, my work, and my family.

I started investing more in my personal growth, and that's when I met the second speaker who changed my life, Jase Souder. He taught me to speak publicly and to have the confidence to be able to do anything by saying "yes" to opportunities, no matter how scary.

Four months into being sober, however, my cousin lost his life to his addiction, and I was ready to give in and start drinking again. Luckily, just weeks later when I was at a speaker training event, I met someone who talked with me about my issues and helped me stay sober.

One of the most memorable speaker training events I attended was held in the Nevada desert. There I participated in an amazing ropes course, where I was able to face my greatest fears.

The plan was to climb up five stories and then zip-line down. Fear gripped me. In 2003 I had fallen twenty feet out of a tree. I sustained a torn rotator cuff, a torn liver, and a cracked wrist. As I stood on the platform, I relived that fall over and over in my head. But then, instead of being frozen in fear, I began reminding myself of what Thomas Blackwell and Jase Souder taught me about positive thoughts and stepping out in faith.

I finally stepped off the platform, went into a free fall, then rode the zip line—and it was simply amazing. In that moment I learned that by fully accessing the power of positive thoughts and being willing to say yes and take a step, I could leave the old me behind and fully embrace the new me.

Another great person I met since getting sober is Natalie. At a speaker training event, she helped me realize the true power of love and what a critical part it had played in my life, pulling me back from the dark side whenever I would slide. She helped me learn how to embrace that inner love and not to worry about sliding back anymore.

I am glad to say that through learning to speak life-giving words, saying "yes," and stepping out in faith and embracing the power of love, the forest of unworthiness in the back of my mind is no longer there.

I now control my life—not the depression, not the anger, not the alcohol.

Amazing things have happened since Mike Crow asked the question that would forever change my life. My business has grown by 35 percent, allowing me to become the largest independently owned home inspection company in my area. I have multiple certifications and am a partner instructor with the largest international home inspection organization in the world.

I have accomplished all these things simply because I first answered the question, "What is keeping you from being the best that you can be?"

That one question allowed me to discover the power of positive thoughts and words and gave me the confidence to say "yes" and take a step. That one question, coupled with the support from my amazing family, friends, and the speakers who have invested in me, has helped me create a life drastically different than my old one.

I no longer feel that I am not smart enough and worthless.

The truth is, I am good enough, I am smart enough, I am worthy, I am letting love lead, and I am becoming the best I can be.

So . . . what is keeping you from being the best that you can be?

Linda Ipaye

Linda Ipaye is a highly intuitive holistic energy healer and teacher at My Best Life Center. Linda specializes in using muscle testing to identify people's challenges emotionally, physically, and spiritually to provide solutions for personal wellness. She also teaches muscle testing to empower people to trust their own energy to learn, heal, and love.

www.idahorealestateshop.com

MUSCLE TESTING, PERSISTENCE, AND A BETTER LIFE

Linda Ipaye

I've always been into nature. I grew up playing in the woods among the spruce trees and princess pines, biking, beachcombing, and caring for our animals. My love of nature led me to learn more about holistic living.

I went to college and started learning about the properties of essential oils and their benefits. I incorporated aromatherapy into my life for relaxation, boosting energy, and improving digestion.

I had our children at home with midwives. Having children deepened my quest for learning to live our life with a more holistic focus.

Muscle Testing for Allergies

When our daughter was about ten years old, there were times when she would have a hard time breathing—for instance, when she played in the grass or ran through a field, especially in the spring when the grass pollen was endless. We went to an ear, nose, and throat doctor who suggested a lot of allergy testing. Based on what I told him her symptoms were, he thought she would need to be on steroids.

Because our daughter had major anxiety about needles, I decided to look for a different solution, so I did research on natural allergy remedies. I sought out a chiropractor that offered an allergy elimination technique.

He used something called muscle testing, which involved my daughter holding an allergen vial in her outstretched hand while he pushed her arm down to see if her energy held her arm strong or weak. If her arm was weak, then she was responding that her body was allergic. If her arm stayed strong, it showed she was not allergic.

I saw the magic for her as her allergies went away. She could play in the grass with her brother and friends and not get congested. She was breathing regularly! She could have fun and not have to stop.

I was blown away. I saw the power of muscle testing on someone else for the first time! It was noninvasive, with no down time and no negative side effects.

Muscle Testing for Menopause

When I was thirty-nine, something was off with me physically. I went to my doctor, and he told me everything was normal. I know myself, and I knew something was not right. I enlisted the help of a friend who did natural healing. She muscle tested me and determined that my estrogen was low, testosterone was high, and DHEA (master hormone) was very low. I was in full-blown menopause! Through muscle testing me, my friend knew what my body wanted, when it wanted it, and how much it wanted for maximum healing.

I experienced the power of muscle testing for myself for the first time. I now had answers to my questions about how to make my life better.

Muscle Testing for a Car Accident and Recovery

One day I was at a stoplight and was rear-ended. I immediately went to my chiropractor. Physically I did not have any bumps, bruises, or broken bones. But a week after the accident, I did a 180-turn in my emotional and mental health. I was crying uncontrollably, couldn't decide what to make for supper, and was depressed. I was not myself.

I was diagnosed with a concussion.

Once again, I went to my friend who did natural healing. With muscle testing, she could tell that the good feeling chemicals were all low. My body wanted serotonin! Muscle testing also allowed me to know when to take it and how much. I continued to get muscle tested to adjust what my body wanted and needed, when to take supplements, and how much to take as my healing continued.

With muscle testing, I have all the answers. I can ask if my body wants something and if so, what is a beneficial amount, and what time of day to take it. Muscle testing allows you to have all the answers to all your questions! It is so empowering!

Muscle Testing for Emotional Healing
A few years later I decided to learn how to use this (magical) tool myself. I wish I could say I just chose it freely, but in reality I sought it out because of another desperate time. My husband had not worked for five years, and we were forced to file bankruptcy. I was feeling a dark, low energy, and I was avoiding my loved ones.

I knew muscle testing could help, but this time, instead of just having it done to me, I decided to learn how to use this tool and gain mastery with it. I wanted it to be available to me at all times.

I started working with experts on muscle testing and how I could learn to be a practitioner.

Muscle testing identified trapped emotions from childhood that I had been carrying. Negative emotions of worthlessness, shock, and hopelessness were released and replaced with positive emotions of worthy, peace, and hopefulness!

Because of removing negative emotions, I regained a positive and bright outlook in moving forward with my life. My husband got a job! My business was doing well. I was spreading light and love!

I now had this amazing tool.

In 2019 our daughter was in college when she was diagnosed with ADD (Attention Deficit Disorder). Instead of freaking out or searching for an expert, I knew I could help her.

We muscle tested to see what would best support her. Was it guidance in organization, sleep, nutrition, supplements, exercise, or something else? There was no wondering and no trial and error.

Using muscle testing we identified the exact support she needed, and she graduated with her PhD.

I use muscle testing in my real estate business. I muscle test home sellers to see if they are ready to sell their home. I use feng shui for the home so the positive energy is maximized to attract the perfect buyer.

Home buyers have me muscle test the home to see if it is a positive fit for their energy. The buyer feels when it is "their" home!

I started using muscle testing with family and friends when they would tell me about things that were bothering them regarding emotions, aches, discomfort, what foods to eat, what supplements to take, which essential oils to use, and what crystals would be beneficial for them. Even questions about the best time to do read, write, be creative, or do detail work can be answered with muscle testing. We really do have all the answers to our questions!

Muscle testing gives you clarity! I've learned that muscle testing also can be used for:

- Releasing trapped emotions, inherited and personal
- How to best be organized
- What to make as a beneficial priority for the day

- Balancing chakras

- Overcoming anxiety

- Choosing the most beneficial exercise

- Balancing your gut

One of my favorite words is *Dharma*. Dharma means what God put you on earth to do. Holistic energy healing is what I was put here to do. Muscle testing is my Dharma.

I use and teach muscle testing to bring people's best life forward. It's my heart. I can't keep that bottled up.

So far it has worked for clients, friends, my family, and myself.

Muscle testing can work for you too!

Jessica Jobes

Jessica Jobes is the co-founder of Mint CRO. Jessica spent eight years at Micro-soft on Bill Gates' "Favorite Engineering Team of all time," where she learned Sprint-Testing, and has coached over 1,000 clients to grow like the Big Dogs. She lives in Seattle with her son.

www.mintcro.com

HOW I LEARNED TO GROW LIKE THE BIG DOGS (AMAZON, FACEBOOK, NETFLIX . . .)

Jessica Jobes

I first learned how to grow online businesses when I worked at Microsoft. We were a team of 3,000 engineers strong, but we weren't just any team. Bill Gates called us his "Favorite Engineering Team of All Time." Our human-driven machine delivered business growth for 49 consecutive months. Every month for four years, we didn't skip a beat. Grow. Grow. Grow.

Not only was our business growing, my career was growing as well. By my thirteenth year at Microsoft, I had learned how to grow MSN and Bing, and I climbed the corporate ladder to the top 5% of this amazing engineering team. Although I wasn't aware of it at the time, the Microsoft growth team I was on was eons ahead of where many of the top growth teams are today, six years later.

In 2014, even though our team was still hitting balls out of the park, I was ready for a change. I left Microsoft and accepted a role as the Studio Director for a hipster web design agency. This agency had techno-vibes galore, and they presented themselves as the cutting edge of the cutting edge.

My first client was Jim, a retired Microsoft VP, who had a new mission to save lives of drug-addicted teens. We were designing a website and an app for the parents of these vulnerable youth. We were so inspired and excited; we were going to heal thousands of families! We had a purpose, and the work didn't feel like work at all.

Finally, after four months, we were ready for the launch. On Sunday night, Jim gave the go-ahead to begin driving traffic to the beautiful new "life-saving" website.

I woke up on Monday morning filled with nervous pride; I rushed to get to the agency early and celebrate the launch with the team. I arrived expecting cheers. Instead, I was met with stoic concentration and zero smiles.

"So far just some website visitors. No sales," I was told.

We fielded emails and calls from Jim, who anxiously asked, "Is everything working? Are you sure?"

We frantically looked for technical glitches, hoping there had been an error on our part. That kind of problem would be in our wheelhouse. We could fix the technical.

But hope of a win faded by the hour, and after two days we finally admitted defeat.

Four months of work and Jim's $80,000 investment had grossed just $900 after the launch.

We all felt sincerely awful. We had wanted the website to be a huge success, yet we failed on so many levels.

Acting under the guidance of the agency co-founder, we presented Jim with the solution: "A social media advertising strategy!"

We pitched Jim on a $94,000 digital marketing plan to grow his business. Jim very wisely said, "Thanks, but no thanks," and stopped returning our calls and emails.

The Client-Guilt was real, and internally I was steaming mad at the agency owners. I wanted to yell at the owners, "THIS IS WHAT YOU ARE SUPPOSED TO BE GOOD AT. You build and launch websites. How could you let us fail so epically and painfully? And then have the gall to ask for more money?"

Little did I know at the time, but this was standard operating procedure for agencies who haven't mastered client growth:

Promise big, fail big, and retain the client for as long as possible.

Pick up a new client by promising big. Fail big. Churn. And on and on.

Unfortunately, this pattern dovetails with a widely shared mistaken belief: If your product and website are great, people will just find it and buy it. The brutal truth is, the "if you build it, they will come theory" doesn't work.

**Lesson #1: "Create a Website and Launch It" does NOT
lead to business growth.**

While it wasn't done maliciously, the web design agency essentially sold sweet-looking cars that couldn't be driven off the lot. The sweet-looking car was the website, but it was missing the engine of high-converting traffic to generate qualified leads and sales.

~~~

When I realized that many well-meaning agencies did not know how to drive growth, I was disillusioned by the industry as a whole. I knew something was very broken and needed to be very different.

I decided to venture out on my own as an entrepreneur and start my own marketing agency. I was determined to find the real answer that would actually help businesses grow.

I tried a lot of marketing approaches very quickly, following all the digital marketing best practices, including testing all the different ad platforms, all the web design tools, building multiple websites, and did a lot of blogging and SEO.

Everything I was reading made sense, and why wouldn't it? All marketing gurus deliver their training with the deceptively simple words, "Do this; it's easy, and it works!"

After six months of creating a lot of content—and driving a lot of traffic to it—I had mastered the art of driving traffic, yet it had only produced 400 leads on my email list . . . and they weren't coming in consistently.

Lesson #2: "Creating content" and "driving traffic" does not lead to business growth.

~~~

I was just plain exhausted, burned out, and it wasn't paying off. I felt trapped on a never-ending "content hamster wheel."

My gut said "STOP! There's still something missing."

I knew success was possible; we had 49 months of consistent growth at Microsoft. Why wasn't it working here?

I wrestled with the question . . . and I found the answer.

While at Microsoft, I relied on data to know if I was heading in the right direction or not.

The data told me what was making our potential customers click, like, share, become a lead, or purchase from us.

Microsoft had millions to spend, and they relied on a team of 3,000 engineers to run 230,000 tests every month to collect data and make decisions that continuously grew the business.

I realized that successful business growth wasn't web design, or creating more content, or driving traffic—it was rapid testing.

Lesson #3: The more you test, the more successful and profitable you will be.

~~~

I needed to test, but how could I test in a way that's affordable to the average business owner?

So I set out to invent a new way to scientifically engineer growth using lots of testing for a low cost—and I used myself as the guinea pig. I'd been following the marketing gurus' advice to use ads to drive traffic, and failing, when I realized I'd been using online advertising all wrong.

I had an epiphany—and discovered the answer to my testing problem:

When I stopped focusing on ad platforms to run ads, but instead started thinking of them as the cheapest, easiest access to run tests with my target audience, suddenly it all got crystal clear.

Facebook had two billion people; any audience I wanted to reach was within reach for only pennies. I didn't need to set up focus groups with a handful of potential clients—I could go direct to the market I was targeting and get hundreds and thousands of data points in minutes. That way, I would know (and not be guessing) what exact messaging and images resonate best with my market. ONLY THEN would I start to use those messages in actual ads on Facebook, Instagram, Google, or anywhere my market was looking and buying.

Essentially I had cracked the code on the cheapest and most trustworthy market research I could possibly find.

I figured out how I could run 200 tests per week all by myself. That's 200 pieces of feedback instead of 1—my speed of learning what the market wanted just accelerated through the roof!

By comparison, consider my previous epic failed launch. We collected no data before the launch; instead of collecting data, we did a lot of guessing about what would and wouldn't work.

We ran one test that took four months and cost $80,000. Now I could run one test in 24 hours for only $25.

As I continued to experiment with new tools and testing techniques, a formula emerged.

I call it the **Growth Playbook.**

It allowed me to increase my testing velocity, and test more ideas, more cheaply on my target audience. Finally I was discovering what worked and what didn't—based on fast feedback.

I went from 400 leads in six months to 10,000 leads in 90 days.

It was down to a science: **1 lead every 8 minutes—just like clockwork!**

Now that I had qualified leads, I needed to turn them into sales.

So I trusted the Growth Playbook again, and after testing my face off for another 90 days, I went from my first sale to a profitable, evergreen webinar.

The system worked. It consistently produced **one sale for every five attendees.**

I completely automated my one-woman business and was able to achieve $35,000/month in revenue.

Lesson #4: The faster you test, the faster you can grow.

~~~

I never wanted to hear another story like Jim's. To make a difference, I knew this was the system that could change the industry and help so many other business owners, so I wanted to share the Growth Playbook.

Instead of starting an agency, I decided to change the industry: no more marketing failures, no more wasted money.

I co-founded a training company for marketers, agencies, and business owners who want to take control of their business growth.

Using our Growth Playbook, we've reached over 1,000 companies, so instead of guessing, they are empowered to make data-driven decisions and create consistent, reliable growth.

To hear the rest of the story . . . go to Erin Athene's Chapter, Engineering Miracles..

Amy Kleptach

Amy Kleptach is the co-owner of a thriving home inspection company in Ohio. Amy has taught at her industry's national convention for three years in a row and has written articles for an inspector-related publication. In her next career, Amy plans to make an impact in the quilting and craft world with her easy-to-make crafts.

amykleptach.com

GIRL POWER

Amy Kleptach

In 2000 I was married to a man I was anxious to call my ex-husband, but I needed to be successful at my career in order to get out of the marriage. I was living and working in Philadelphia, Pennsylvania, selling pizza menus for an eccentric entrepreneur who called himself "The Cowboy." As his only salesperson and to gain instant respect with the pizza shop owners, I called myself "The Cowgirl" and wore a cowboy hat on sales calls.

One sunny afternoon in January, I was driving north east on I-95 toward New York City. During the hourlong trek, I got an urge that I could not brush off. I needed a drink to keep moving down the road—I needed to fill my Snapple bottle with liquor!

In New Jersey, there's a Package Store on almost every corner, so I pulled into the closest one and went inside to make my purchase.

Feeling relieved, I sat in my car with the liquor bottle in my hand. I poured half of my iced tea out and was about to replace it with the alcohol. Holding that bottle, preparing to pour, I had a thought: *If this is what it takes to get down the road today, what will it take tomorrow? How about the day after that? Will I need a drink then as well?*

I put the bottle down. Without drinking a drop, I turned the car around and drove home, making a promise to myself that I would have a new job by the end of the week.

After just three interviews, I secured a position in sales with a merchant services company. I would have to learn how to sell to make money, but I was up for the challenge. I knew there would be a great future for me when I learned how to sell.

Training at my new job consisted of three evening classes from 5:00 to 9:00 p.m. The first night of training, a blizzard hit, but that did not deter me. I made it through the snow and learned as much as I could in class. Traveling home that night, it was snowing heavily—and then my car had a flat tire. "Girl Power, Girl Power, Girl Power" was the mantra that enabled me to get the tire repaired and get home safely that night. It seemed that if something bad could happen, it would. I remember thinking, *This isn't going to stop me. I need a new future!*

The first day on the job, I was clueless. I wasted the company's good sales leads! By the second day, I hated the job. I didn't understand sales; I didn't realize that I was offering a fantastic service for my customers. It was so bad that I even called one of the companies that had turned me down for a job and asked them to reconsider.

Cloudy, cold, and about to snow again is the best way to describe the weather that afternoon. My appointment was with a custom jeweler. Sitting in my car, preparing my sales plan, as I had just learned, a man wearing a winter coat and holding a bag of salt emerged from the jewelry store and stepped onto the sidewalk. He locked the door and began to apply salt to the sidewalk. I remember thinking, *Amy, this is your prospect who just locked up his store and is about to leave.* At that moment, I had a choice: to take the easy route and let my prospect get in his car and leave, or get out of my car, get this guy back in his store, and make myself some money!

My hand landed immediately on the door handle! The business owner and I went inside to talk about how credit cards could make his business a lot of money. My delivery was choppy, but I hit all the key points in my presentation, and with the help of my sales manager, I closed my first sale!

By the next morning, the sales process was clear in my mind. I now understood the sales process and the need for the steps. I saw a future for myself!

When my first paycheck arrived, it was one of the best moments of my life. My one-week paycheck was two and a half times the amount I previously made for *two* weeks. I was hooked on sales. I understood, I was a believer, and I was incredibly excited for my future.

I spent the next eight years perfecting my craft. On my lunch break I would read and memorize rebuttals so I could easily overcome prospect objections. I developed stories to make a substantial impact and sell my product. I won sales contests, including an all-expenses paid trip to Nassau's Paradise Island! I even taught my brother how to sell, and he became the best salesman for ten years in a row at his company. My passion for sales never died, and it has led me to sharing sales and marketing techniques with others through classes and coaching.

Life is great now. I make my own work schedule. My husband and I are able to travel regularly. More importantly, we have a succession plan and a plan to fund our retirement with our business. When I think back to those critical growth years, I think of them fondly and cherish the experience and lessons learned. They helped me to understand that I can be more than the status quo, and that hard work does pay off. It helped me to get to my "why" and connect with what would ultimately fulfill my life.

I believe that everyone can be an entrepreneur. I believe if you have the right training and skills, you will be able to create profitable opportunities for yourself, to be successful, and to live the American Dream. And I believe we can do this while treating one another with kindness and respect. Most of all, I learned that Girl Power, determination, and the sheer desire to grow and take a step forward every day will lead you where you desire to go. Dream big—and keep on keeping on!

Dave Koshinz

Dave Koshinz is a teacher, coach, and entrepreneur. He built and sold two businesses while traveling a personal growth path through yoga, meditation, group work, neuroscience, movement practices, psychodrama, and shamanism. He now helps people have better lives by sharing what he has discovered through his personal life journey.

www.davekoshinz.com

WINNING IS THE ONLY OPTION

Dave Koshinz

I first learned about personal responsibility as a teenager. One warm summer day, my brother brought me to a used bookstore. The old, run-down shop was a maze of bookshelves stretching to the ceiling. It seemed the scene contained every topic I could imagine, and many that lay beyond. Suddenly a massive amount of knowledge, wisdom, and information was at my fingertips.

As I explored the many aisles, a set of bookshelves marked Yoga and Philosophy drew me in. I flushed with excitement as I looked through the esoteric tomes.

Just cracking various books open and reading random pages, I felt such a deep connection with the knowledge. It felt like the essence of their teaching was being downloaded into me. Something in me changed as I instantly embodied the intention of the words.

That day I learned the world is richer and more profound than I had thought possible. And each of us is so much more than we ever could imagine. I was introduced to philosophies that had the power to shape my world. The books told me I could master my life. Instead of being its victim, I could take charge and really own my life.

By being fully responsible, I could master myself—and by mastering myself, I could change my world. I had found a key puzzle piece to who I was, and I knew this was the way for me. There was no other option.

Walking into that bookstore, I was an angry teen and a troublemaker living on the edge of self-destruction. Walking out, I found my way forward to healing and crafting a life well lived.

Even better than knowing that I could change my life, those books showed me the practices that could make it happen.

That day I learned I could change. I began learning how, and I started the practice of changing. I realized that life is based upon my personal responsibility—and when life isn't working, I have to work on the key factor: me.

Soon after I started working for a couple who were into personal development. They spent much of their free time at personal growth workshops. Their favorite was known for its emphasis on accountability. I was intrigued and signed up for the next training.

This workshop had gained a reputation for making people angry. Sure enough, I thought all the helpers in the training were mean, and I was irate.

These assistants were very direct, unemotional, almost robotic. It seemed as though they were trying to make us angry, and the thought of that made me angry. I had fallen into a mental loop of sorts.

The trainer talked about personal responsibility and how we perceive things, making decisions based on our beliefs, assumptions, and interpretations. I put that together with how I was feeling and realized I was making assumptions about the assistants; I realized I was responsible for how I saw them. I worked on shifting my attitude toward them, but it felt nearly impossible. On the last day of the training, they became polite and started interacting with us, which drove home how dramatically my assumptions, interpretations, and beliefs had affected my perception. Suddenly I liked them, and we had a good laugh about the whole thing. That moment my commitment to personal growth and responsibility deepened profoundly.

Everything I learned from the books and the training prepared me for the challenge of building successful businesses, including the tech company I just sold, which had grown to thirty-five employees and millions in revenue.

Thirteen years into that business, however, I allowed myself to drift far from these important lessons. I lost track of my core beliefs and practices.

That year my business was reeling from the loss of our largest client, and we were in an industry downturn. After letting go of half my workforce, I was burned out and ready to give up. The bank had frozen both my business and personal credit—all my wiggle room was gone. Already I was grieving the loss of my business, thinking that its death was imminent. Obsessively thinking through the problems brought but one answer: bankruptcy.

I recognized the downward spiral I was in and knew that I needed some radical change. I was invited to a rite of passage workshop and signed up without hesitating.

The first night of the workshop, we were rudely awakened at 1:00 a.m., divided into teams, and sent off on a scavenger hunt. Our team, in a fit of misguided enthusiasm, waded waist-deep into a pond.

As I walked out of the pond, icy water dripped down my cold legs and pooled in the grass. I stood there in a field with thirty other men, shivering, while anger welled up in my stomach.

We thought we were going to capture one of the flags in that pond, but instead we only got cold and wet. I felt like we had been tricked into making a logical yet wrong choice.

I desperately tried to find someone to pin my misery on, someone other than me, that is. I was playing the blame game and looking for someone to throw the blame at. Who could it be?

The guy who invited me to this crazy workshop?

Maybe the guy who thought going into the pond was a good idea?

Perhaps the guy who woke us up in the middle of the night?

Then it became clear. There was one, and only one, person responsible for me being cold and wet: me. I walked willingly into that pond.

I connected that moment with what was happening in my business, and the penny dropped. In my business I was busy looking for who to blame while shirking my responsibility and my role in how things had gone bad.

As I stood shivering in that field, the new realization sunk in and I remembered I had been there before: blaming someone else for my problems. Under the stress of my business, I had drifted back to old ways of thinking that kept me from clarity and decisive action. Once again, I wasn't taking full responsibility and had gotten myself stuck.

During the scavenger hunt I had held back, not speaking up when I questioned the wisdom of our foray into the pond. I chose to trust someone else to make the right choice rather than be responsible for my own wisdom. It was just like in my company when I held back and hedged my bets.

As we headed back to the lodge to change clothes, I started considering my life from a place of greater personal responsibility. I thought about what had happened and what needed to change.

Looking outside for the problem and assigning blame wasn't working. I was standing in my own way. Years earlier I had gotten out of my way and made dramatic changes through personal responsibility, daily discipline, and living intentionally—and I could do it again.

I committed to personal responsibility on that cold, wet walk back to the lodge. I had definitely been losing before, but now winning became the only option.

I decided to make a list of principles that would support the new me, the winning me. Seven came to mind, and they have become cornerstones of my life.

1. Take personal responsibility.
2. Practice daily discipline.
3. Live intentionally.
4. Learn from passion.
5. Step into fear.
6. Lead with curiosity.
7. Question my beliefs, assumptions, and interpretations.

My lead principle is taking personal responsibility; it is the flip side of blame. When I'm responsible, I'm not blaming anyone, including myself. I recognize cause and effect, but I don't let blame get in the way of learning.

Getting clear on these seven principles grew my confidence, and I started feeling like a winner. I set my intention to turn my business around NOW.

My positive and confident mindset fueled my decisions, and I started taking clear, bold steps.

Living my principles led to shifting my focus from the downturn and what I had lost to what I could do with what was currently true. I could never go back to what was, only forward to what could be. I took responsibility for the loss, let it go as a learning experience, and focused on creating the future I wanted.

Once my mind shifted from losing to winning and I right-sized the business, we started making a small profit. My team was re-energized, with a clear plan to bring the company back to full health.

Living my principles was key to turning the business around within the year. Years later the sale of my company gave me the freedom to start my next venture: passing on the life-changing gift of personal responsibility. I now share the wisdom I've gained by coaching and mentoring leaders to live the seven principles and take personal responsibility so they can turn things around and live inspired lives.

Natalie Lavelock

Natalie Lavelock, RN-MSN, is a sought-after program development specialist and online business strategist who works with professional coaches and speakers to create lucrative coaching programs, courses, and certification programs that allow them to scale their business and fully live a life they love.

www.natalielavelock.com

TURNING TO FAITH

Natalie Lavelock

I sat at my desk in nursing administration, staring at the skylight. Trying to feel the calming warmth of that single ray of light descending into my office, I could feel the conflict arising within me. It was an unsettled stirring that seemed to be signaling a change on the horizon. At first I didn't understand. What was God trying to tell me? I mean, by all external measures I had it all. I was near the top of the corporate ladder. I had the trust and respect of both the hospital administrators and my colleagues who worked at bedside. What was there to change?

Have you ever felt that way? Have you ever felt, deep in your soul, that something big was about to happen, but you didn't know when or why?

As the feeling persisted, I started exploring other ways I could create even more impact within the organization through the programs and trainings I was creating and implementing. In doing so, I began exploring the world of coaching. I decided to take a course so I could be a better trainer for the organization and create better programs for our patients. The course took about four months to complete, and I was excited to implement what I had learned!

Toward the end of my training, both the hospital CEO and the Chief Nursing Officer (CNO) decided to retire. They were an incredible team to work with, and Lynne, my CNO, was not only an exceptional leader, but also had become a mentor to me over the past couple of years. So when these two leaders announced their retirement, I was both elated for them and heartbroken for me. This must have been what I felt coming those several months ago.

Wrong!

Shortly thereafter, the new CNO was hired, and within just a couple of weeks, my boss said she wanted to have a meeting. No big deal; we had regular meetings all the time. It was no secret she was hoping I would take her position as the director of Women's Services for the hospital when she retired.

But on that day her whole demeanor was different. As she walked into my office and sat down next to me, I could see the distress on her face. She sat down and said, "I have something I have to tell you, and I hope you'll consider my offer."

Wait . . . what? What are you telling me, and what offer?

She proceeded to tell me that the new CNO had decided to eliminate my role within the organization as the Clinical Nurse Educator. Instead they wanted me to move into a management position to assist my boss in her role running multiple departments.

I wasn't quite sure how to feel. Honestly, I was just trying to sort out the words I had just heard. On one hand I was in shock. I thought of all the things I had done for the organization: creating a whole new revenue-generating service line, fast-tracking a four-year-long accreditation process to become the fourth hospital in our state to achieve a Global Designation, developing a Nurse Residency Program to decrease staff turnover, not to mention all of the staff training and patient education programs—and they're just "done" with my role?

But on the other hand, I was elated because management *was* the next rung on the ladder and now finally within my reach—what an honor! My boss proceeded to tell me that I had the long Labor Day weekend to think about it, but she needed an answer by Tuesday. No rush, you know—just make a quick little decision on something that would change the ENTIRE trajectory of my life in seventy-two hours (insert rolling eyes emoji)! The only thing I can remember muttering to her in that moment was, "I'll think about it."

As I left work that day, not sure whether I wanted to skip and cheer or cry my way to my car, I started thinking about what this new role would mean for my family. Having worked for this organization for over fifteen years, I knew the ins and outs of most of the "admin" roles. I was thinking to myself, *Oh man, this means a new "title" and a raise! I've waited for this for so long! But it also means more time away from my family . . . being on call 24/7/365 . . . getting called in to work on holidays, nights, and weekends when there was a hole in the staffing schedule, even after working a forty-plus-hour week.*

Suddenly, this "promotion" opportunity felt more like a death trap! I had three little boys at home; they were a precious gift from God, and I knew I only had a short time with them to do the job that no one else could ever do: be their momma. And that began to tug at my heart.

But what other choice did I have? Quit my job?

So, as we always do on Labor Day weekend, my family and I headed to the lake. That entire weekend I fasted and prayed, trying to discern what God wanted me to do. Believe me, I truly felt like I was in labor that weekend! And as I wrestled with the decision to be made, Satan took the opportunity to create as much confusion and fear as possible. He gave me thoughts like, *Are you really going to throw your career away? What kind of mother would put her children at risk—no income, no insurance, no retirement—you're going to lose your home and your children are going to starve. Your children are going to hate you. Do you really think your marriage is strong enough to handle this?*

And the whole time I heard God saying, "You get to choose. You can choose prestige, the 'safety and security' of a job, or you can choose to step out in faith and follow me. You can learn to depend on me and watch what I will do."

Let me tell you, that weekend was EXCRUCIATING! Seconds felt like hours, and every decision felt like it was life or death.

But I knew one thing to be true: I wasn't going to let fear rob me of the opportunity to follow God and experience the goodness of what He had in store.

So with all the courage and faith I could muster, I walked into that hospital Tuesday morning, shaking all the way, and told them that I would be resigning and that I would NOT be accepting the offer to move into the management position.

And it felt GOOD!

For about five minutes.

Then I realized that I had to find a way to make money—and fast! Living in a rural area, jobs like mine were practically nonexistent.

I started to think about what I could do. I thought about what problem I could solve and how I could help others and earn an income doing it. Then I remembered my training as a coach. I started looking at how to start a coaching business and questioning if this could be a possibility for me.

I discovered that:

- People who were good at social media taught others how to do social media.

- People who were good at fitness taught others how to get healthy and lose weight.

- People who were good at public speaking taught others how to get good at public speaking.

And that's when I realized: You can turn your expertise into income.

But what was my expertise?

As I thought about it, it hit me! My expertise is helping others turn their expertise into income by creating coaching programs, training programs, information products, and online courses that could help them make more money, help more people, and make an even bigger impact in the world!

Since that time I've been able to build a business that allows me to do the things that are most important to me, all while helping others to make a bigger impact in the lives of those they are called to serve.

But it never would have been possible if I had chosen comfort and security over stepping out in faith to do what felt like the impossible.

And I'm here to tell you: You can do it too. Whatever that big, scary thing is that you've been called to do, choose to say "yes" to walking in faith—and see what God will do!

Albert Lu

Born in Texas and raised in the suburbs of Southern California, **Albert Lu** brought his talents and experiences to the Treasure Valley of Idaho in 2017. Living in Boise, he delivers high-level fitness and health coaching to help others in his community become strong and independent contributors to society.

www.idahomemovement.academy/coaches

A PASSION TO MAKE A DIFFERENCE

Albert Lu

I knew that I had more to give.

I was working as an entry-level scientist, and I wanted more. . . . I had a desire to serve and lead. I hoped to effect true change in people and our country, and so I went through a long, intensive application process to attend Air Force Officer Training.

When I found out I was selected, I had a sense that this new career path was going to help me do more for others. It was exciting.

Because the military heavily emphasizes physical fitness as a foundation to be a warrior, and there are standards to follow and comply with, I knew I needed to "get in shape." A university classmate of mine was in ROTC, and I saw a photo of him doing CrossFit. When I asked him about it, he said, "Come to class."

I will never forget my first day of CrossFit—it was October 17, 2011.

The final part of the class consisted of us students competing against the clock. A fourteen-pound medicine ball does not sound menacing, but after a few repetitions of such a full-body movement, the assault on the body's senses and machinery turns into a war of attrition.

Every single part of my body hurt when the clock stopped. My heavy panting and my heartbeat consumed my hearing as I lay down on the mat, forming my first sweat angel. As the volume of the loud music faded, although I was writhing on the ground in muscle-burning pain and my head was spinning chaotically, I was somehow at peace. On the drive home, my arms felt so heavy that it was a herculean effort to turn the steering wheel.

I was hooked.

While it was hard, I kept going; it worked, and I got in better and better shape. I kept going until the day I left for Officer Training, where I scored the maximum points possible on the Physical Fitness Assessment.

The second Friday night of Officer Training, we were awaiting further instructions from our upperclassmen after they had just put us through an intense, high-stress knowledge and procedure testing session.

I was putting away clothes and gear and was studying our operations manual while my roommate was resting on his bed. I felt a dull pain growing sharper by the minute in my stomach.

The pain was excruciating enough that I decided to leave our dorm room to get help. So I called out to my resting roommate, "Hey, I'm in pain . . . I've got to go . . ." I was in so much pain that I went against the instructions we received to stay in our rooms, and I opened the door and stepped out into the hallway.

It was just after 9:00 p.m., and I was taken by ambulance to the ER where I was put under anesthesia in order for the doctors to see what was wrong. It turns out I needed emergency surgery to repair a perforated duodenal ulcer.

I woke up early the next morning lying in a hospital bed with three tubes connected to me: an IV for pain medication, a catheter to help with urination, and an Ewald tube to pump my stomach.

That was bad enough, but the worst was seeing an open wound about five inches long running from up above, around, and below my belly button. At that moment, I felt utterly helpless.

I went from scoring the maximum points possible on the Physical Fitness Assessment, to being bedridden, barely able to move without feeling pain.

Talk about a gut punch, literally. It didn't seem fair; here I was in great shape, and something over which I thought I had no control derailed me.

I spent a week in the hospital recovering. I spent another week on base to continue to recover. My dream of serving took a hit when I learned I was going to be medically discharged.

I was assigned to a dorm room by myself, and I began to plan my trip back home. In my room, I could still hear everything that was going on. My classmates were still going through training, and I could hear their motivational cheers, commands, and general interactions.

Knowing I couldn't continue to train with them, and knowing my dream was derailed, I sat in my dorm room and cried.

I felt left out. I was completely depressed at that moment. Life sucked right then. My future seemed uncertain and bleak. I had met and interacted with some of the best people I had ever known, and I wanted desperately to be part of such a high-performing community. It hit me at that moment that I couldn't keep following my dream of serving and leading.

I was medically discharged and found myself back home recovering from the surgery and getting back into shape.

That summer I spent many long hours in self-reflection. I realized that the ulcer wasn't out of my control; it was my wake-up call telling me that I needed to change how I saw the world, how I saw myself, and how I lived my life.

I realized the ulcer was the result of years of being too hard on myself, too rigid. It was the result of years of poor eating and drinking habits and too much self-imposed stress.

I realized that on the outside I was like a Lamborghini, but on the inside I was breaking down.

I knew I needed to clean up what I was doing. It wasn't just the food; I needed to change myself as well. I needed to remake myself from the inside out.

I boiled it down to four things I needed to change: the way I thought, felt, ate, and moved. I needed to have a better mental outlook. I needed to be more relaxed; I needed to slow down. I needed to improve my nutrition and drinking habits, and I needed to learn to move my body correctly.

I was on a path of not only healing myself from the injury and surgery, but also preventing it from ever happening it again.

About a year and a half into my healing journey, I decided to take on the challenge of teaching and coaching others.

I still had the desire to lead and serve, but now, instead of leading and serving in the military, I could lead and serve by helping people change their lives by changing the way they thought, felt, ate, and moved.

A passion to make a difference in people's lives grew in me, and I knew if I wanted to help others, I had to keep growing. I delved into self-development, attending seminar after seminar, course after course. I applied the knowledge I gained to my own mental, physical, and emotional health.

I started to intern with my CrossFit coach, learning how to teach and coach others to improve their fitness and health. Through coaching CrossFit, I was able to pass on the knowledge I was gaining, and I was helping others to turn their lives around.

While attending a nutrition conference, I was fortunate enough to meet someone who gave me the book *Rich Dad Poor Dad* by Robert Kiyosaki. This book ignited in me a desire for independence, and my biggest takeaway was that I could start my own business.

I realized that the best way to fulfill my goals of leading, serving, and changing lives could happen through owning my own business, and I would enjoy the benefits of business ownership.

After a short time of running my side business while working in an office full-time, I realized, "I could do this on my own."

I had taken my health into my own hands, and now I was making a commitment to take my work life, my mission, my finances, and my future into my own hands. I wanted to make sure I could leave the pressures of corporate America forever.

I made a commitment to myself that I would get out of the rat race and create a business that would allow me to be self-sufficient by helping others be self-sufficient and healthy, mentally, physically, and emotionally,

I decided to make a move, literally.

I quit my job, packed up my truck, and moved to Boise, Idaho, to fulfill my mission.

Moving to Idaho and starting my own business has afforded me the chance to live my own best life—and to pass it on.

I established Idahome Movement Academy, where we are in the middle of creating a movement. We are on our way to a life of thinking, feeling, eating, and moving better.

I am proud of the impact we are making here; our tribe is amazing, and life is good.

The future is bright. We are on our way to living free

Troy Olds

Troy Olds is passionate about teaching his clients the principles and strategies they need to optimize all areas of their lives and reach the next level. He shows his clients how to take control of their mental and physical states so they can increase energy and feel better than they ever have before.

www.tragictomagic.com

TRAGIC TO MAGIC

Troy Olds

One night, feeling the pain of my recent divorce, I picked up a drink and flushed years of sobriety down the drain.

For the next three years, I tried to claw my way back to sobriety. I was exhausted from the start, stop, start insanity of addiction. And then I received "the call":

"I need you to meet me at St. Luke's Emergency Room, NOW."

I could hear the chaos in the background—yelling and what sounded like someone being restrained.

My son had taken a massive amount of LSD, and in his hallucination, had gone into other people's homes to find some safety. A homeowner who always has fast access to his weapons nearly shot my son. The sheriff who arrived on the scene nearly shot him too.

All of this . . . on my watch (or lack of).

I had shared the "good times" stories with my kids but left out the consequences. Big mistake.

I picked up the phone (instead of a drink) and called my friend Lorenzo from my twelve-step program. "Lorenzo, I need help."

He immediately drove in from two towns away to sit with me in the hospital.

Then I called Jessica.

"Jessica, I need help. I've been lying to you guys. I've not been sober. I've been showing up to meetings and lying about my drinking. Carson is in the emergency room, and I'm f-ing scared. Will you please talk to me while I get to the hospital?"

And she helped me.

"I'm sick of your shit, Troy . . . DECIDE!" —God

I left the emergency room and went back to the room Carson and I were renting from my friend Margo and started packing our things.

I was back in time to watch Carson wake up from the sedatives that finally kicked in and allowed him to sleep. The look on his face when he realized where he was, when he realized that the night before had not been a dream, hurt my heart. I saw his eyes; I saw his spirit break. There are no words.

We left the hospital. He got in the car, head low, several felonies hanging over him.

The pain of addiction is something that is difficult to describe. To be driven by something and have no control is terrifying, confusing, confidence shredding. To pound the steering wheel, crying because it was going to happen again, yet still drive to the dealer's house, is a loss of control that I can only describe as Hell.

I wanted out. I wanted my son OUT of Hell.

I looked over at Carson in the passenger seat, and I knew it was a crucible moment.

I might lose him with what I was about to say.

"Carson, we are moving into Grandma's spare room. I need you to get a sponsor and go to ninety meetings in ninety days."

Carson rolled his eyes. My body tensed, and I could feel my heart pounding in my temples.

OK . . . God, I need your help.

I looked at him again. "Carson . . . I need you to get a sponsor and go to ninety in ninety—or get the fuck out."

I held my breath, waiting for him to answer.

There was a long pause as he looked at me. "OK, Dad."

I went back to the fellas in my men's group and told them everything and asked them to help me. And they did.

Carson and I moved in with my sweet mama. I stopped any attempt at working and making money. Instead, Carson and I went to work on our number one priority: getting straight and getting straight with God.

We went to two twelve-step meetings a day for over three months and then daily for a year. (I still attend my men's group over Zoom every Monday.)

Carson and I slept in the same bed for five months. I wasn't letting him out of my sight.

We'd wake up at 5:30 a.m. and drive twenty miles to the 7:00 a.m. meeting. Afterward I'd get him to probation and then back to the other side of the valley so he could finish his classes. In the evening we'd go to the 6:00 p.m. or 8:00 p.m. twelve-step meeting.

I dove back into the rituals that healed me the last time. Breath work. Meditation. Cold showers. Journaling. Reading. Prayer. STEPS.

Carson busted out his inner creative and made a forge; he created amazing art made of molten metal.

As he forged his creations, God and the program forged us into better men.

He picked up his knitting needles and began knitting mittens and hats for our twelve-step friends.

One morning in the middle of winter, we woke up for our meeting, and when I started the car, it was nearly on empty.

"Carson, we have enough gas to get there, and that's our job—to get there."

It was a much needed lesson to be humbled and raise my hand and tell the group we needed gas money to get home.

After the meeting, my friend John gave us a hug and told us to meet him at the gas station. There he filled the tank of our car.

The people, the meetings, the steps all filled our spiritual bank account.

See, I was the guy who wore the right clothes, told you about my past successes, name-dropped the people I knew, and NEVER let you know what was really going on in my life. EGO—my ego THOUGHT it was protecting me. But what it was doing was keeping me from a true connection with others. I HAD to let YOU see in so I could see out. Thank you, Emil, for that saying. I use it often.

Those times. Those meetings. Those people. The shitty coffee. The sobriety tokens. The shares. The friends. They all are priceless memories.

THE most painful, scary, and humbling time in my life transformed into the most precious, priceless experience of my life.

Very few people know me—my thoughts, my history, the fears I carried—like my son now knows me.

He was part of our men's meetings, and he learned that it is OK to ask for help. That we all have pain. That we all feel alone at times. That there is a SOLUTION! That good men can share their hearts, can love and support one another. That human beings need one another.

Time to Work
We were getting our car's gas tank filled. We were filling our spiritual bank accounts. Now it was time to get back to work and earn some money.

I can feel the chair I was sitting in in the upstairs room of my mother's house. I can see Carson knitting away in the chair next to me. My mind was dancing around, wondering how I was going to pay child support and the penance of my past, when the phone rang.

My friend Albert Bradley was on the other end; he needed help painting one of his properties. Ten bucks an hour.

I looked at Carson. "You in?"

"I'm in!"

"Let's go!"

An hour later we were taping, painting, and listening to podcasts.

We did our best. We made an impression. Albert's partner Stephen owned a bunch of Papa Murphy's, sold them, and was now flipping properties.

Stephen is a GOOD man. And Stephen had lost his wife a year earlier to an overdose.

When the property on Harrison Blvd was finished, Stephen, Carson, and I went to lunch, and I shared with him my vision of "Wellness Basecamps" where people could come and receive the love, support, tools, and resources to heal their brains and bodies.

Not just addicts and alcoholics would be welcome at Basecamp. Everyone was welcome.

Stephen put up the seed capital to get Ascend Wellness Basecamp launched. Now we just needed clients.

Well . . . having turned my will and my life over to the care of God, God called me—disguised as Daryl Hill. Daryl was at Matt Bacack's mastermind, where he met Jase Souder. Jase was saying to Daryl, "Wouldn't it be cool if there was some place that entrepreneurs could go to heal themselves, get healthy, AND still be able to work?"

Daryl grinned. You see, I had JUST spoken with Daryl about Basecamp A COUPLE OF DAYS BEFORE!

Jase Souder was my very first client.

By now Carson and I had moved into our friend Albert Lu's home. He's a Cross-Fit coach and an amazing human. With the gym on the property and plenty of space for cooking and classes, it was perfect.

Jase flew out and stayed with us for two weeks. He extended his stay for another twenty-one days. He flew out for an event. Then he CAME BACK for a while longer. Finally he decided to move to Idaho. And he has become one of my closest friends.

Carson and I got sober on November 1st, 2017.

We held our first Ascend Wellness Basecamp on May 7th, 2018.

Redemption

It was incredible to be in the courtroom as the judge looked at Carson's file and to hear him say, "Son . . . I've never had a person who stood in front of me who took care of business the way you have. You've gone above and beyond to make this right. I think you had a really bad night, and I believe you've learned from it. . . . I'm expunging your record, and you are free to go."

Things move fast when a person is mainlining God. Whatever your concept of God, listen to it.

Since that time I've been called to work and create from the Island of Hawaii. My YES to that call has opened many doors.

My team and I work with clients virtually and are preparing for our next Basecamp.

We teach what we've learned over twenty years of seeking out the best coaches and mentors, and we continue to invest in our own personal growth so we can share with others and they can learn to live their best, most vibrant life.

We do intervention work for families dealing with addiction, and at the time of this writing, I assist Tony Robbins with his coaching and training programs.

Our experience is not to be hidden. We don't shut the door on it as if it didn't happen. It did happen. And to regret it is to diminish its value and power to help others.

Life is a journey. Every experience brings lessons. If you are going through hell, keep going. Get help. Because nothing changes if nothing changes, and we are all EXACTLY where we are in life by our own creation. It's time to create something great!

Christine Rothdeutsch

Christine Rothdeutsch combines her bookkeeping background and love of details with her leadership roles in various volunteer organizations to assist frustrated, overwhelmed, and overworked solopreneurs. When she is not behind the computer screen, you can find Christine speaking on how you can have a successful business and not be harnessed to a nightmare.

www.implementingyourvision.com

HOBBYIST OR BUSINESS OWNER? FINDING YOUR KEY TO MAKING THE SALE

Christine Rothdeutsch

Working, doing a good job, and getting paid a good wage has always been my belief since my first job out of high school. Every job I held prior to starting a family included promotions, more responsibility, and more pay. But none of those jobs were building a career for me.

Then I became a stay-at-home mom.

We always lived comfortably, but managing our future financial picture never happened. My background is in bookkeeping, not managing the finances. Money comes in; money goes out.

Contributing to the household finances was always in the back of my mind while raising two children and managing the household. But how? Then an opportunity for a part-time job appeared. By this time my daughter was in the fourth grade, my son was in second, and both were doing well. I thought it was time for me to step away from family management and back into the workforce.

For the next seven years, I held a few jobs on and off while managing our household and family. Throughout the years I also volunteered with several parent organizations, rising to the role of president in several. The last one was almost a job, but I learned so much. If you have ever had a child in middle school band, you know what I mean. As president for two years of the school's band and orchestra parents club, I met with the band director every day. There were many activities to manage, and every year we took the students on an overnight trip—six busloads of students, teachers, and parent chaperones. And we never lost anyone.

Another time, not knowing what to do after being let go from a position at a local small business owned by "friends," I found myself sucked into a network marketing company. It was partly because I felt I wasn't safe anywhere if "friends" didn't value me enough to keep me on.

At that stage of my life, I didn't think I had anything of value to offer an employer—at least not enough value to earn more than ten dollars an hour. And we still didn't have any retirement savings. The only thing we were building was credit card debt.

One evening, I hit bottom. I was depressed about having spent so much money on network marketing when I had nothing to show for it. Well, I did have a bit of product in the closet, but no team, and no income. I found myself crying hysterically to my husband.

The kids were in high school by now, and I had given up any possible career I might have had before having kids. Going back to bookkeeping didn't feel like a viable option. I wanted something more, something different. I wanted and needed to earn big money so that I wouldn't wind up on the street in my retirement.

Sometime after hitting bottom, a friend pointed out that I was good at keeping meetings on track and productive. She told me that I was into the details and other things that small business owners needed. I said, "Great, but no one will pay me," and she said, "Yes, they will." With her encouragement, I decided to start my own business as a part-time office support specialist, working for multiple businesses at the same time.

I believed that as soon as I hung out my shingle, my schedule would be filled. That's not quite how it happened. It was difficult explaining to local business owners how they would benefit from my help. I would be out networking several times a week, meeting lots of people for one-on-ones, aka get-to-know-you sessions. Still, not much work came my way.

Then I met a business coach. She worked specifically with virtual assistants. I benefited somewhat from her short coaching program and then was introduced to another type of coach. This next coach was all about getting clients. Yes! That's what I needed. At the end of her three-day event, I decided this was where I had to be. Her yearlong program was what I needed if I was going to go from a hobbyist to a business owner. I spent two years working with her. I learned about marketing myself, but I still did not have a clear description of what I did for clients. There were still some missing pieces.

Spending more money with that coach was out of the question, and so I was on my own. It was time to take what I learned and figure things out myself. It sounded like a plan at the time.

Over a year later, as a birthday gift for myself, I attended a business conference. This one was all about business building. And I got to fly there. Oh, what a birthday present! After three whirlwind days of meeting new people and learning a lot, I signed up for another yearlong coaching program. This time I knew I was in the right place. Everything I learned so far from the event was methodical—do this; don't do that. Start here if your business is in the early stages or start at another point if you're an established business. I felt this was my last opportunity to build a real business or I'd have to get a job.

What I learned rather quickly is that in order to get clients, I had to ask. Ask for a call, ask questions, and ask for the sale. Simple, right? Not really.

If I wasn't clear on how I specifically helped clients with their technology, then I couldn't get prospects to understand. Over time I discovered numerous and evolving descriptions and messages about my business. Each time I thought, *This is it! This is what I do.* I say each time because my services changed only slightly over the years, but as I brought on new clients and they had different needs, my messaging changed.

Raising the level of my services each time led me to the service package I had been looking for—something that encompassed all of my marketing, tech, and operations skills. I realized that I am the marketing and operations organizational specialist for my clients. I help them to weed through the noise, decide what they need and don't need, and implement their systems to get clients.

The moment I sold my highest-priced monthly package, I knew I had arrived. I went from playing small (hobbyist) to playing big (business owner). It took me many years, many programs, many digital tools, and many dollars.

I was always second-guessing myself and my value. Now I'm think, *Why didn't I do this sooner? Why didn't I present this package sooner and ask for the sale?*

Over many years I've learned that:

- Hanging out a "shingle" doesn't get me clients.
- When clients don't make money, I don't make money.
- When "business owners" don't make a profit, they can't help people with their knowledge.

I learned exactly what I needed to do to get clients. I was able to weed through the noise of all the choices out there, from coaching programs to self-directed programs to tech tools. I was able to establish the systems I needed to get high-paying clients. And that is what I do for my clients.

There is a lot of noise out there. So many tech tools, coaching programs, self-help books, etc. If self-help books really worked, would there be so many available?

And jumping from one program to another when you don't understand what it is that you really need is a poor decision.

When you weed through the noise and take the exact steps to make sales, you too will ask yourself, *Why didn't I do this sooner?*

Jase Souder

Jase Souder is a nationally recognized speaker and trainer, specializing in public speaking and sales. Jase has appeared on national and local TV and radio and is featured in the inspirational movies *Pass It On* and *The Power of Coaching*. He has been published in multiple books.

www.worldclassspeakeracademy.com

THE BEST PART

Jase Souder

The first time I spoke and sold my own seminars and coaching, I made ninety-eight thousand dollars in sales. The second time I spoke and sold my own seminars and coaching, I made about four thousand dollars. The third time, I made about forty thousand. The fourth time, I made just a few thousand.

Then one day, I made zero.

That doesn't mean I broke even; I had to pay for my own travel and expenses, so I lost money. But losing money wasn't the worst part.

What was worse is that I had no idea why I sometimes crushed it and sometimes sold nothing. The big sales days were great; taking home tens of thousands of dollars from one speech tided me over the times when I sold poorly, but the ups and downs were frustrating. There was no continuity, and my confidence started to take a beating. But even that wasn't the worst part.

I started my career working for one of the best speakers, and I watched him sell from the stage over and over again. When he finally gave me a shot, he said, "You've seen me do it enough times. Go do it." That literally was the extent of my training.

I got a copy of his presentation and attempted to memorize it word for word, but it was his speech, so I couldn't duplicate it exactly. I couldn't tell his stories either; that would have been inauthentic.

The first time I spoke and sold his stuff, I did ninety-six thousand dollars in sales. But I didn't have any idea why it worked, so the next time I did under fifty thousand in sales, and then the next time even less. I had no idea what I was doing.

Next I started selling my own seminars, and I worked at getting better. I paid one guy four thousand dollars just to learn to close. I paid another guy twenty-five thousand dollars to help me write a presentation. I invested a lot of money, but there still was no consistency. But even *that* wasn't the worst part.

When you're selling from stage, as I was, the promoter gets a percentage of your sales. At that time, the standard was 50 percent, so if I sold forty thousand dollars in seminars, the promoter would get twenty thousand. Promoters look at their guest speaking slots as revenue-generating opportunities, and if there were little-to-no sales, it costs them money. If one speaker could make them twenty thousand dollars and another makes them zero, it's a big difference. So, if a speaker sells poorly, the promoter isn't happy. But that's still not the worst part.

Promoters are part of a tight network, and they talk. If a speaker bombs on one stage, the promoters tell the other promoters to stay away, so bombing on stage costs the speaker the opportunity to get on other stages. Yet even that wasn't the worst part.

One day I spoke at an event where I'd spoken previously and hadn't done too well. I wasn't confident. I still couldn't count on my speaking to generate sales; I didn't know what made it work. I just hoped that if I was on, excited, and resonated with the audience, they'd buy.

I did my best—and made zero sales. I was disheartened and out a good chunk of change since I'd paid for travel and lodging for my assistant and myself. The promoter sent his assistant to take us to dinner, and I thought, *Oh, maybe the promoter told his assistant to give me a pep talk.*

The promoter's assistant was acting awkwardly, and about halfway through the meal, he looked at me. "We'd like to invite you . . ." he said, and then after a big pause, "not to come back."

That was the worst part.

I was embarrassed, I was hurt, and I was a bit ashamed. I'd put my heart and money into learning to get better, my speaking was about something very important to me, I wanted to make money, and more importantly I wanted to make a difference for the audience—and now I was invited not to come back.

That stung, and I was worried that the word would get out that I bombed, and other stages would disappear.

I had to do something about it, so I kept signing up for speaker trainings, investing in leadership and development trainings, and working on my craft, but my sales stayed inconsistent. Until the recession—when all sales stopped.

The market for my seminars and coaching was real estate investors. I was teaching them personal growth and one-to-one sales. I'd mastered one-to-one sales, but that doesn't translate to one-to-many. When the recession of 2007 happened, the real estate market dried up fast, and the demand for training real estate investors disappeared.

While this was devastating to my business, it turned into a blessing for me. Suddenly I had a lot of time on my hands.

I was thinking and praying about how I could continue to serve people and make it more affordable and effective for them to learn. I decided to take the best of my $2,500 seminar and create a home study course on sales.

I had been teaching sales for years, and I wanted to get even better. In order to make the best product I could, I threw myself into learning sales. I started reading more sales books, watching videos, and binging on TED Talks. I spent hours watching these talks on YouTube.

The talks that really impacted me were the ones on social dynamics and psychology. I learned about what creates lifelong fans and clients, what triggers unconscious social networks, and what causes masses of people to take action.

About this time, I had the desire to figure out a system for speaking. I asked myself, "What am I doing when I rock? What am I not doing when I bomb? How can I consistently make sales?" I realized the principles I was learning about sales, social dynamics, and psychology could be applied to writing speeches and presentations that move people to action.

I combined my learning, experiences, and training and created a system—a framework for writing high-converting speeches. I realized that there are a series of yeses we need to get from the audience in order for them to purchase from us. It's like there are a series of light switches, and they must all be switched into the on position, in the correct order, in order for the light bulb to go on and our audience to say yes to our offer.

To make sure all the switches were on in every presentation, I created a repeatable system I could follow to write my presentations. It wasn't a template of words or sentences to say—instead it was a series of discussions and stories to tell in order to activate and move the audience.

Soon after I finished producing my home study course on sales and creating this framework for speaking, I was given an opportunity to audition, or "try out," for a big stage. The audition came with a catch: I wasn't allowed to sell. The promoter put this in the contract and kept saying, "Remember, you're not allowed to sell."

The day for the audition came. I used the template, and I rocked the presentation. The audience was engaged; they laughed, they were inspired, and they gave me a standing ovation.

At the end of the presentation, the promoter walked on stage and whispered in my ear, "Let's sell your stuff."

I replied, "I thought I wasn't allowed to sell."

He said, "You rocked it; let's sell your stuff—we'll give them a discount."

We sold my home study course, and that one day's sales, even after discounting the price, equaled 25 percent of my previous year's sales!

After the event, the attendees left and the promoter asked me to sit and talk. After a couple minutes of small talk, he looked at me and said, "I'd like to invite you . . ." My heart felt like it stopped. I thought I did well; I thought he'd be happy. The last time I heard that phrase, it didn't end well. Then he continued, ". . . to speak to my group four times a year; I'll pay you a monthly retainer to do it, and you can sell your stuff every time, including being on stage at my big three-hundred-person event."

Using the system I created, I spoke at his big event, and that one day's sales equaled 50 percent of my prior year's income. With two speeches using my new speaking system, I made sales equal to 75 percent of my previous year's income, and I spoke on his stage for the next seven years.

I've gone on to speak on multiple stages, create hundreds of thousands of dollars in sales, and impact hundreds of lives.

That was the best part.

Marshall Sylver

Marshall Sylver is the world's leading authority on subconscious reprogramming and irresistible influence. Combining entertainment, education, and empowerment, he weaves an enchanting process to change millions of lives worldwide. Whether he is on TV or live on stage, it is certain he will bedazzle. Enjoy his raw, real, and uninhibited direction to make your life what it was meant to be—a life of adventure rather than a life of maintenance.

www.sylver.com

LIKE A BAT OUT OF HELL

Marshall Sylver

So this is hell. I am being attacked by the government, threatened with twenty-seven years in prison for an offense I didn't commit. I am going through a divorce from an eleven-month marriage; the divorce is lasting four years. Due to Nevada law, I am paying for my attorney's fees, my soon-to-be ex-wife's attorney's fees and thousands of dollars in monthly spousal support to an ex who never contributed a dime to the relationship and is having a relationship with the marriage counselor we were seeing. I am dating the girlfriend from hell, whom I have discovered is not only cheating on me—she is also going into my safe and stealing thousands of dollars in cash from me. I am crying my eyes out daily to my COO, only to find out that because I am in such bad shape, she is embezzling over $1,000,000 from me, right under my nose.

Do you want to trade places? What would you do if you were in my place? Seriously, what would you do?

Fast-forward: I am sitting in a gorgeous home right on the beach in Southern California. The house is worth 10 million dollars, and it's just a vacation home. My main residence is a 17,000-square foot palace in Las Vegas that sits on 1.5 acres with a 125,000-gallon pool, a tennis court, a skateboard park, a putting green, and more. I am flying around the world exclusively on private jets, changing lives.

My businesses have done over half a billion dollars in transactions. I am driving a Rolls Royce while in Vegas, a Mercedes Maybach while at the beach house. I have a net worth in the many millions. I am married to the most perfect woman. Our relationship is better now than when we met fourteen years ago. I have three totally awesome children who bring me massive joy every single day. I am happier than I have ever been in my entire life. I literally have EVERYTHING I want.

What did I do differently?

I found Certainty.

My intention in this chapter—and the intention of this book overall—is to help you have a Phoenix story: rising triumphantly from ashes to a life beyond anything you ever dared to dream. No matter where you are right now, there is a path to get to where you want to go. There is a way to win the game that is different from how you have been doing it, and it works.

Be Certain.

If you are on your last breath, rejoice.

If you are doing OK and long for something better, rejoice.

If you are doing really well, rejoice . . . rejoice. Starting this very moment, everything changes to a supernaturally charged life that I guarantee you have not comprehended in your past as your birthright.

I am Marshall Sylver. The two opening paragraphs are a fact. My childhood was equally as challenging. I was born and raised on a farm in Michigan with no running water, electricity, or telephone. My family was homeless in a cold Michigan winter when the local community converted an old chicken coop for us to live in. I have ten siblings, all birthed by my mother. I am the seventh born and have no recollection of any father figure ever living with us. We were dirt poor, and we barely survived. Very early I learned the lesson that if our lives are to be anything, we must take 100 percent responsibility for our outcomes and choose to be victors rather than victims.

It all starts with Certainty. Certainty is the absence of doubt. Certainty has no hope, wishfulness, or positive mental attitude attached to it. It's a fact, it's done, and it's Certain.

Often people don't know how to turn their lives around. They are so far down that the idea of ever being happy, let alone living the life of their dreams, seems absolutely impossible. That's the reason you must start with Certainty. When you are Certain, you finish things. When you are Certain, you stay in good spirits. When you are Certain, you look for the victories around you. Since what you focus on expands, you will find what you are looking for when you are Certain.

Sometimes things are so tough, and then the first thing you have to do is to surrender. Surrender and find your life perfect, because finding it less than perfect is a waste of your time. To surrender is not a loss; it's just the opposite. To surrender is one of the most powerful tools of transformation. When we surrender, we can enter Satori. Satori is to live in the present moment. To be here now.

Surrendering allows you to take inventory. To acknowledge that whatever you were doing doesn't work is humbling. Sometimes surrendering can be momentarily humiliating, but your ability to surrender puts you in complete control in the long run. When you find your life perfect, you ask different questions. "What's good about this?" "That door is closing for a reason; what door is opening?" The ultimate understanding is when you decide you are going to tell God the plans you have for your life, and God just laughs. Here are the powerful steps to helping you go from doubt to absolute Certainty.

First, as I said, is surrender. Denial doesn't cure. If things suck, then they suck. I promise you that not everything sucks. Take score, figure out where you are, then start thinking about where you want to be.

"Are you broke? How broke?"
"Are you lonely? How lonely?"
"Are you unhealthy? What's unhealthy?"

After you have surrendered and taken inventory, ask yourself the hard question. It's a question that cures much. It's a question that can stop arguments in their tracks. It's a question that can give you instant relief and instant inspiration. What is the question?

"What do I want?"

Notice it doesn't ask, "What don't I want?" That's the wrong question. Since what we focus on expands, you can never get what you want by identifying what you don't.

Financially, what do you want? "I don't want to struggle" emphasizes struggle. "I want one million liquid net in the bank" is very specific.

When you ask for exactly what you want, you begin to get clarity. You will see through the garbage and let go of the drama and useless energy wasters. When you have a massive definition of purpose, you let go of time wasters and toxic people and simply focus on advancing what is important. When you have a clearer understanding of what you want, only then can you eliminate what you don't.

The next step is to compartmentalize and put out one fire at a time. Once you start putting out the fires one at a time, your life will get infinitely and incrementally easier. You likely cannot solve everything in one fell swoop. Solve what you can and surrender for the moment to what you cannot.

You are a vessel, a water glass that is constantly being poured into—by your family, friends, mainstream media, big tech. You must pay attention to what is being poured in. Is it poison? Is it pure drinking water? Most people, when they find their lives are going well, are fairly full of poison. It's OK. Change is Certain.

Reality is created by validation. When you seek change in your life, a useful strategy is to find people who have gone through what you are going through and are successful.

As I get ready for open heart surgery, I have sought out others who have gone through it. I have asked them about their experience and how their lives were positively impacted. You can do the same regarding your relationship, finances, life challenges. Others have gone through what you are going through and have been successful. There is a way to win that is different from how you are doing it, and it works.

For things to change, you must change. The world is unfair. The world doesn't care about you. It's not required to. Getting angry at the game or the way life works is foolish. I know it's very Zen, yet it is what it is. That is a fact.

Your Phoenix story is right now. Rising from the ashes to be bigger, better, and more than you ever dreamed has started as you read these words. In this very moment, be transformed in the twinkling of an eye. The world is a better place because you are here. You are a gift to the planet.

You must take total control of your thoughts and emotions. You choose every single one of them. Nothing has any power except the power you give to it. What you believe to be true is true for you and nothing else.

Choose to be Certain at this moment. Be Certain that you matter. Be Certain that you are here for a much bigger reason than you know. Be Certain that whatever challenges you are going through right now are for your own good and are designed to make you better than you ever thought you could be.

There were times in my life when it was really hard to find perfection in my circumstances. Even now, as I prepare for surgery, I absolutely would rather not be in this situation. Sometimes putting things in perspective helps. I am going to the hospital by choice in my own time. Not in the back of an ambulance. Not after collapsing at the gym. My perfect wife is going to drive me, and not some random stranger hired to do so. After surgery, I will be stronger, more energized, and have more longevity than ever. It's all good.

Be here now; surrender to what is. Utilize versus tolerating the circumstances of your life. When you do that in all areas, you will start to create so much prosperity that there will only be one thing left to do: serve others.

My prayer is that something I have said in this chapter has resonated with you. My desire is that it brought you some peace and Certainty. I hope that you said, "My gosh, his life was really screwed up. If he recovered from that, I can handle what I am going through."

Yes, you can. No matter what is happening right now, I promise you it is temporary. This too shall pass. It's just a bump in the road.

So many times I worried way more than was called for. So many times what I thought was horrible was actually really good. So many times, I thought I had a better plan, and God just laughed.

On that note, have a sense of humor. Not only does funny mean money—laughter really is an amazing medicine. My household laughs. We laugh out loud. We laugh often. We laugh at one another, and we definitely laugh at ourselves.

Very soon that which you have cried over, you will be laughing about. Human beings are motion junkies. To feel alive, we create motion in our lives. When we don't think we can create positive motion, we often subconsciously crash our lives to have an experience of rebuilding.

Get out of your head. Get into other people's lives by being of service. Ultimately, the less you make your life about you, the easier it becomes. In my darkest moments, the ability to help someone else brought me the greatest joy and kept my own challenges in perspective.

You are not alone. Together We Got This. #TWGT. It's a glorious life filled with love, health, opportunity, and potential. It's our choice every single day to find the blessings. Thank you for choosing me.

You are loved.

Dale Troy

Dale Troy, college success coach, is the founder of Crush College Stress, a company dedicated to helping students succeed in college. Dale is a graduate of Yale College and Yale Law School, and the mom of three Yale College graduates. Dale teaches students habits and skills to create a positive academic experience.

www.crushcollegestress.com

COLLEGE LESSON: GET HELP FROM AN EXPERT

Dale Troy

I had dreamed of going to college for many years. It was going to be the best four years of my life; so I had heard. And I was excited to be going to my dream school, Yale College.

I prepared carefully for the new adventure. I bought dorm bed sheets, new clothes, shower supplies, notebooks, and highlighters. I also wrote to my roommate to decide what we would each bring for the room. I brought a rug and a standing lamp. She brought a small chair and a mini fridge. It was going to be great.

Classes started out well. I was an A+ notetaker, and I knew that was key for me. I began meeting people in my classes and made lunch dates with some. I tried out for the Yale Dancers—and made it! College was going well, and I even began thinking about law school.

About a month into my freshman year, I started having severe headaches and nausea. I missed some classes, which I hated to do. A few times I became so dizzy from the headaches that I had to stay in bed. When I called the health center and described my symptoms, I was told, "It sounds like migraines." The nurse instructed me to take Tylenol, drink water, and rest until the symptoms went away. I followed her advice, but I felt nervous, not knowing when I might have a migraine again. It was unpredictable.

At about the same time, I started feeling nauseous even when I wasn't having a migraine. What could that be? I had no idea. Throughout high school I had complained of stomach pains and had seen a gastroenterologist. Every test they put me through came back negative. I was diagnosed with IBS (irritable bowel syndrome). There seemed to be nothing I could do to prevent it, so I didn't bother going to the health center when my stomach issues cropped up again.

My dad told me to eat Tums, which is what he relied on for years for his "sour stomach." I became a Tums eater too. I ate them before meals, before classes, and before bed. But I still felt nauseous often.

I remembered that pregnant women were told to eat crackers and bread when they felt nauseous, so I added those to my daily routine. Unfortunately, the Tums and the extra bread didn't make the problem go away. But I didn't let how I felt stop me from studying in the library every day and making sure I was well prepared for each quiz and exam.

I became very conscious of where the bathroom was located in every building I entered. I chose a seat near the door in every classroom. I sat at the end of a row in a lecture hall or a movie theater. I never actually got sick, but just having that horrible feeling made me want to be prepared for the worst.

I also kept a small brown paper bag folded up in my purse. The bag was a security blanket, in case I really got sick at an inopportune moment. It never happened.

And I never told anyone how I was feeling either.

Why? Because I had become convinced that no one could help me, nor would they understand what I was going through. I kept it all to myself.

Meanwhile, I focused on my classes, meeting people, studying in the library, and going to dances on the weekends. Dance was my one escape. I loved to dance—both as part of the Yale Dancers and as a regular college student looking to have fun, and maybe even meet a boy. I was determined not to let my physical issues get in the way of doing well and enjoying college. My goal was to go to law school like my dad and my grandfathers, and nothing was going to stand in my way.

Fast-forward to my senior year. I was still having migraines and nausea, but I had also collected a large number of As in my classes, and my goal of going to law school was looking very good. I just had to stay focused on my goal, believe in myself, and trust that my physical symptoms, though very uncomfortable, would eventually go away.

I wasn't prepared for my next physical problem. I was in my dorm room, and all of a sudden, I felt like I wasn't breathing—like my heart was going to stop. I felt my pulse, and it was there, but my brain was telling me that I couldn't breathe. I started sweating profusely. My roommate saw me and insisted we go to the hospital.

I don't remember what happened in the hospital—only that hours later, they sent me "home," back to my dorm. Apparently, I had been hyperventilating and that was causing me to feel like I wasn't getting enough air. Yikes! Could it happen again? Yes. What should I do next time? Breathe into a paper bag. LOL—that wouldn't be a problem since I always had a paper bag in my purse!

Although I hadn't told my parents how difficult it was to function with migraines and nausea, I decided to tell them about my trip to the hospital. But I wanted to do it in person, so I drove home.

As I sat in the kitchen of my parents' home, tears welled up in my eyes. My mom and dad cried as I explained in detail how hard it had been for me to be a straight-A student while dealing with constant physical problems.

"I feel so helpless. I don't know how to help you," my mom said between her tears. I knew my parents would do anything they could, but there didn't seem to be an easy answer since I had already been to so many doctors. I didn't intend to make them feel responsible; I just wanted to be open about what I was going through.

I actually felt relieved after opening up to them. No more secrets. Just knowing they understood me better made me feel supported. On campus, I had been keeping everything a secret. I wanted to fit in. I didn't want people to look at me differently. And I was determined to follow through with my plan to go to law school, which meant doing well in my courses despite how I felt physically.

Looking back, it almost seems like an impossible task. *How did I do it?* How did I continue to push myself? How was I able to graduate summa cum laude from Yale while dealing with migraines, nausea, stomach aches, and panic attacks?

A couple of days after meeting with my parents, I got a call from my mom with some "good news." She gave me the name of an allergist, an expert in helping people find the root cause of a problem when no other doctor could figure it out. He had a system of testing for food and environmental allergies that would take a number of months, and his success rate was impressive.

Of course I said yes! I was ready to start. I would drive from Yale to his office forty minutes away, no problem. Suddenly I had a reason to be hopeful. My mom and I cried tears of joy over the phone.

I began my journey with the allergist by having weeks of testing. The next step was to eliminate foods and substances that I was sensitive to. Afterward I did the elimination diet, which required me to eat only one food at a time and record how I felt.

It was a long, arduous process, but I stuck with it, trusting that this expert knew what he was doing and could help me get rid of my uncomfortable physical symptoms. Finally, three months after starting the process, I began seeing changes in how I felt. The light at the end of the tunnel had appeared.

What carried me through all those years before I found the expert who could help me? My inner strength, which had developed over years of not feeling well, allowed me to proceed toward my goals. Looking back, I see how valuable habits, discipline, and optimism were in helping me overcome my challenges at college. That realization became the basis for my five-step method of helping college students.

Now I'm the expert. And I help college students learn how to succeed in college, no matter what challenges they're having.

Jeff R. Wilcox

Jeff R. Wilcox is a family man, a lifetime multi-preneur, certified small business consultant, venture capitalist, public speaker and facilitator. He is passionate about serving those who are dedicated to bring abundance into their lives by turning obstacles into opportunities and weaknesses into strengths. He is available at jeffrwilcox6s@gmail.com.

jeffwilcoxspeaks.com

GETTING RID OF THE CLUTTER

Jeff R. Wilcox

I'm standing at the edge of one of the most beautiful, unexplored canyons in the Pacific Northwest. My wife, Joanne, is by my side, and we are the only two people in sight. A thousand feet below us is a beautiful river that over the years has cut an oasis through the desert landscape. As we take in the majesty of such a view, I reflect on the series of events that have transpired over the past ten years and the miraculous transformation of abundance that has infused every aspect of my life. Truly, I stand amazed and humbled by the evidence of such abundance: Joanne, the love of my life, seven amazing children, three grand-children, the blessing of an early retirement, the money in my bank accounts, the peace in my heart, and the love that permeates my surroundings. How did I get here?

We all have events in our life that we misinterpret because of our own fear and ignorance. Oftentimes we allow the litter of our mistakes to clutter up our future and keep us in scarcity. We allow our ego to lead instead of allowing joy, peace, love, hope, serenity, humility, kindness, benevolence, empathy, generosity, truth, compassion, and faith to lead the way. My clutter was feeling displaced, unworthy, robbed, betrayed, and dismissed.

When I was three years old, my parents adopted a little five-year-old girl—my new sister. This caused me to feel displaced.

As a child I remember ducking behind bushes and running past certain bully-occupied houses so I could avoid the onslaught of jeers and physical and emotional attacks. I felt unworthy of being protected and that it was somehow OK that I was being bullied.

When I was eleven years old, I became addicted to saving money. I had a pint-sized Tupperware container that was made to look similar to crystal with prismatic indentations. I received my allowance for doing my chores one week and put it in this container, and I liked the way my two dollars looked all rolled up. I found a quarter in the couch; I saved my lunch money; I put my birthday money into the container. I counted my money every day; I really enjoyed watching the amount grow. I had exactly $18.35—more money than I had ever touched in my life. I loved the sound of the coins rattling in the container. I decided I was going to be wealthy.

Nothing was going to stop me—until the day I was standing by the kitchen counter and saw my mother's best cutlery knife laying on a cutting board. Next to the cutting board a pencil was randomly placed. So, as a typical energetic boy, I grabbed the pencil and the knife and started whacking the pencil on the cutting board. About the time I was getting into a good rhythm, my father walked into the kitchen. Even though there was no harm done to the knife, and pencil cost less than a quarter, my father was furious. His eyes bulged, and his voice confirmed that I was in big trouble. "Do you know how much that knife costs?" he said in that "angry dad" voice. "You are going to have to pay for that." I know he was trying to teach me a lesson about taking care of things, but as I handed over the container, what I was really learning or hearing was "Even if you work hard for something, you will be robbed of it." In my mind's eye, I recall holding up the container like an offering to the gods and having it swiped from my hands as though I wasn't worthy of such things. From that point until well into my adult life, having money was something I always struggled with. I lost $18.35 when I was eleven, and I felt robbed. There were several occasions in my career where I saw hundreds of thousands of hard-earned dollars slip through my fingers.

After seven years of marriage, having been a better-than-average husband, a good father, a good provider, etc., I was betrayed by my wife and soon divorced. I lost my home, and it seemed as though I even lost my children. I had done everything in my power to have a happy family, and now I felt like even that dream was being dismissed.

Why was it so easy for me to be displaced, abandoned, robbed, betrayed, and dismissed? Why did I work so hard for something only to have it taken away? This clutter led me into addiction, self-loathing, and a life full of scarcity. In 2010 my net worth was a negative $250,000. I was angry, I was losing money, and I wasn't enough—there wasn't enough. I wasn't someone I wanted to be around, and neither did anyone else.

The Turning Point: The Sanctuary, the System, and the Source

Some call it coincidence, but I believe coincidence is God's way of trying to stay anonymous. Well, it happened that at my lowest point, I was introduced to a true gentleman, a very wealthy man who needed desperately some of the skills and abilities that I had honed over the years. It was hand in glove. To say he was rich would be an understatement, but there was so much more surrounding him than just his money. I had the opportunity for a few years to work in an environment where I interacted with him on a daily basis. He never formally gave me advice or coached me, but he taught me volumes on how to operate a life full of wealth and abundance.

The Sanctuary

First, he showed me how to live life peacefully. Working with him was like being in a sanctuary. He did this humbly, by avoiding any egoic tendency. He was not driven by his ego. He didn't get caught up in being less or more than someone. He felt he wasn't any more deserving than someone else, nor was he worried about how he might be seen. When I fell into comparisons, he helped me see how I was choosing war over peace.

The System

Gratitude

This man constantly thanked me for the value and improvements I brought into his life. As it turns out, gratitude is among the highest emotional vibrations you can emote. If I was leading with the wrong emotions, I would do like he did: I would find something I was thankful for and express it.

Generosity

He was wealthy—and he wanted everyone else to be wealthy. He knew that wealth wasn't something you hold on to; it was something you allowed to flow through you. He would say to me, "I want you to be a wealthy man." He would give generously to me financially, energetically, and timewise. This allowed me to give to others. And the more I gave, the more I realized nothing was really mine.

Alignment

He would never give negative thoughts more power by putting them into words. He believed that everyone and everything around him would bring him benefit. I learned from him that alignment simply is lining up your thoughts with your desires.

Attraction (Attitude of Action, Faith)

He was very flexible in how things got accomplished—but stubborn about how things were going to end up. He wielded unflappable levels of faith. He would speak to things so passionately that they seemed to materialize right in front of my eyes. He was a very faithful man; the principle of faith is a principle of action and of power, and by faith he would command the elements to manifest abundance into reality.

Receiving

This is the most difficult part of creating abundance and wealth in one's life. When you show gratitude, give generously, and align your thoughts with powerful action, you would think everything would turn out in order, on time, and without delay. Well, it's kind of that way if you are willing to receive what is manifesting in your life as though it were a gift— even if on the surface that is scary.

The Source

It was Einstein who posed the question: "Do you believe the universe is a friendly universe?" How you answer will determine the outcome of your life. If there is an all-powerful entity or being that wants you to thrive, it would make sense to connect and partner with such a powerful energy. My mentor showed me that having a partnership with the most powerful being in the universe allows us to have the energy to be at peace and put effort in the necessary steps. Without a connection to that energy, ultimately we would suffer under our lonely and solitary efforts. He was religious about connecting with his Source and maintaining that relationship. This is where his inspiration, energy, and passion came from. Once he had that, everything else fell into place.

How blessed I am to have been around a man who had very little clutter. And how miraculous it was for me to be able to see his processes. It gives me so much confidence to know that what I allow to clutter my view is truly my choice. The level of wealth and abundance I can have in my life is also my choice. And it is the same for you!

Joanne Wilcox

Joanne Wilcox is a mother of seven, a professional organizer, an energy coach, and the creator of the L.I.F.E Archetype personality assessment system. Joanne is passionate about helping people see their perfect love and worth by understanding the way the Lord created themselves and others.

lifearchetype.com

UNDERSTANDING THE NEW STRANGER SO, WHO ARE YOU?

Joanne Wilcox

My Story

Ever since I can remember I've wanted to be a wife, dental hygienist, and a mother. That's pretty much what happened. Of course, our marriage was not as "happily ever after" as I'd planned, but whose is? I chose to make lemonade.

It wasn't long before my husband and I had nothing in common. Not even our faith. When I was eight and a half months pregnant with our fourth angel, my husband told me what he'd been up to, that he had chosen a new lifestyle and wanted a divorce.

Have you ever lost your identity? Not on paper, but in your soul? I did. I will share with you how I reclaimed it.

If I wasn't a wife, who was I? When my little treasure was born, I was suicidal. My perfect little son needed me, and oh, how I needed him. He truly saved my life.

My body, mind, and soul ached to such a terrible state that I had a grand mal seizure. My neurologist said it was from overstressing and not drinking, sleeping, or eating. I weighed eighty-five pounds—that's about sixty pounds below my normal weight. I was not OK in so many ways.

		L.I.F.E Practical Personality Profiling	Joanne Wilcox 208-870-7832

auntiejojohelps on Facebook, Instagram, Pinterest. Email at auntiejojohelps@gmail.com

Joanne Wilcox
208-870-7832

	LOVING	INNOVATIVE	FUN	ENLIGHTENED
Summary Term	Curving	Active	Bubbly	Still
Face Looks	Soft features. Curves. Oval face shape & eyes. Long eyebrows.	Asymmetrical. Triangles. Pointed. chiseled. Cleft chin. Warm. Earthy.	Round. Circles. Youthful. Freckles. Dimples. Cute. Bright. Smiles often.	Oval or rectangle. Parallel lines. Consistent skin color. Hight contrast skin & hair color. Striking.
Movement	Slower paced. Smooth. Supportive. Quiet.	Faster paced. Side to side. Aggressive. Loud.	Faster paced. Bouncy. Inclusive. Random.	Slower paced. Precise. Methodical. Quiet.
Speaking	Soft. voice flows gently. palms down. hand gestures, small slow movements. Slow inflections almost monotone. Holds own hands. Touches person talking to. Likes oodles of detail. Head tipped to side. Nods yes while listens.	Loud. Uses quick strong hand gestures. Aggressive sound effects. Pointed inflections. Hand on hip. Pointed finger. Likes bullet points not much detail. Head up or down.	Animated. uses lots of hand gestures. Palms up. Voice inflections, sound effects, high pitched voice. Touches person talking to. Smiles & giggles when talks regardless of message. Hands moving most of the time. Head moves around.	Quiet. Little movement with inflections or hands. Will not talk to fill space. Very concise. Leaves hands at sides. Head straight. Speaks with exact pronunciation. Only speaks if has something important to say.
Primary Motivation	Comfort	Results	Happiness	Respect
Decision making	Research. 2nd 3rd opinions	Quick. Rarely regrets decision	Goes with gut. Little detail	Analyzes & researches
Possible Strengths	Loving. Friendly. Steady. Understanding. Deep. Patient. Cooperative. Amiable. Relaxed. Sincere. Calm. Affectionate. Peacemaking. Curious. Observant.	Innovative. Ambitious. Competitive. Passionate. Direct. Motivated. Practical. Dynamic. Confident. Daring. Adventuresome. Persistent.	Fun. Positive. Inspiring. Popular. Pleasant. Social. Spontaneous. Charming. Trusting. Confident. Vibrant. Persuasive. Bubbly.	Still. Thoughtful. Precise. Bold. Mature. Cautious. Organized. Clear. Vivid. Patient. Dependable. Detailed. Analytical. Prompt. Finishes. Neat. Thrives on having direction.

	auntiejojohelps on Facebook, Instagram, Pinterest. Email at auntiejojohelps@ gmail.com	L.I.F.E Practical Personality Profiling		Joanne Wilcox 208-870-7832
	LOVING	**INNOVATIVE**	**FUN**	**ENLIGHTENED**
Possible Limitations	Lazy. Difficulty in prioritizing. Dislikes change. Yield to avoid controversy. Stubborn. Indecisive. Can get stuck preparing. Second guesses self. Worry.	Lack tack & diplomacy. Acts too fast. Loud. Intense. Aggressive. Inflexible. Domineering. Impatient.	Impulsive. Inattentive to details. Late. Situational listener. Gullible. Exaggerator. Distractable. Unorganized. Messy. Forgets.	Can get stuck in analyzing. Prone to depression & moodiness. Overly intense. Icy. Know it all. Be defensive. Procrastinates.
Contribution to Team	Dependable. Cooperative. Empathetic. Logical. Service oriented.	Creative. Makes things happen. Challenge oriented. Motivated. Makes things entertaining/ fun.	Creative problem solving. Cooperative. Diplomatic. Motivating. Enthusiastic.	Maintains high standards. Objective. Conscientious & steady. Analyzes all data for best result. Comprehensive problem solver.
When Stressed	Inflexible. Indecisive. Unconcerned. Sarcastic	Pushy. Ego driven. Demanding. Aggressive.	Self promoting. Talkative. Unrealistic.	Fussy. Picky. Overly critical. Pessimistic. Quiet.
Emotion when Triggered	Non-emotional.	Anger.	Overly optimistic.	Fear.
Thrives in	Predictable & stable environment that allows time to change. Long term work relationships. Little conflict. Freedom from restrictive rules.	Innovative & action/future oriented. Non-routine. Challenging. Ability to express ideas and opinions. Independence. No controls or details.	Wants to be heard. Freedom from detail & control. High amount of contacts. Democratic supervisor with whom can associate. Freedom of movement.	Small group. Familiar work environment. Private work area. Technical work or specialized areas. Where critical thinking is needed.
Doodles	Soft waves. Loops. Connects. Swirls.	Hard pointy edges. Angles. Explosive. Active. Triangles.	Stars. Hearts. Arrows. Swirls. All upward yet random. Likes to fill in spaces.	If any doodles: straight lines. Parallel. Symmetrical. Enjoys blank/white spaces.

	auntiejojohelps on Facebook, Instagram, Pinterest. Email at auntiejojohelps@gmail.com	L.I.F.E Practical Personality Profiling		Joanne Wilcox 208-870-7832
	LOVING	**INNOVATIVE**	**FUN**	**ENLIGHTENED**
Colors	Soft. Greys. Cream. Rose. Seafoam green. Spring colors.	Warm. Brown. Rust. Hunter green. Earthy. Autumn colors.	Bright. White. Navy. Pink. lime green. Cheerful. Summer colors.	Pure. Clear. Black & white. Liberty red. Kelly green. Winter colors
Fabrics	Flowy. Soft. Comfortable.	Textured. Heavy/substantial. Lots of movement.	Light. Lots of movement. Trendy.	Quiet. Still. Fairly classic/formal.
Patterns	Plaids. Florals. Lace. Ruffles. Various sizes. Low contrast.	Large patterns. Animal print. Camo. Plaids. Random. Loud. Asymmetrical.	Small whimsical patterns. Hearts. Stars. Shapes. Flowers. Arrows. Random.	Symmetrical. Parallel. Stripes. Polka dots. High contrast.
Metals (jewelry)	Brushed nickel. Silver.	Oiled bronze. Copper. Gold tones.	Shiny gold.	Shiny silver.

My Turning Point

Then a miracle happened. I remember it so vividly; as I was carrying laundry up the stairs one day, I turned and saw my reflection. The woman staring back at me was consumed with rage, fury, and bitterness. She startled me so much that I dropped the laundry basket and fell to my knees, crying. I could NOT allow that image to continue to be the way my children saw me. As I knelt there praying, I felt angels wrap me in love, understanding, and support. I pled with the Lord to change my heart, to help me learn how to love myself. I'd put all my self-worth in what my husband thought of me. I had given away my identity and my self-esteem. That was my mistake. In that moment I claimed that responsibility and intentionally chose to recover my self-worth.

I felt like the woman I wanted to be was a stranger. Did I like her? Who was she? Author Laurel Hamilton said, "The only true happiness is knowing who you are," and after my divorce, I went on a crusade to rediscover myself.

I did a myriad of personality tests to learn who I was, to discover my strengths and weaknesses. The tests had several things in common. Each described four classifications of personalities. The attributes in each classification were similar yet different. There are many profiling systems to choose from. Each can help you gain an understanding of yourself and others. Each system has strengths and limitations.

The biggest limitation I encountered was interpreting and applying the test results to be useful in my life. Then I wondered: What if tests weren't necessary? What if our unique inner qualities were connected with our outer features? In other words, if you're naturally bubbly and joyful, you will naturally have a youthful energy—no matter your age. Likewise, if you're naturally more serious, you will have a sophisticated quality in your appearance. Not because you *will* it to be this way, but because you were *built* this way. I completely geeked out about personality types and research. The following chart is the result of all my studying, answers to prayer, and soul searching. I call it **LIFE**.

The data looks at your strengths, weaknesses, modalities, motivations, and tendencies. It contains your walking and talking styles, as well as your physical features. It addresses your decision-making style, primary motivation, words you like to hear, the way you behave when you are stressed or triggered. It includes what colors, patterns, fabrics, and jewelry metals compliment you. It even examines your doodles!

As with everything, there are those who discount the effectiveness of the data. However, there is adequate science and psychological evidence to prove its value. The reality is that it's 95 percent accurate. Because this method uses divinely created physical traits that do not change, the results don't either. Consider these references:

Give instruction to a wise man, and he will be yet wiser: teach a just man, and he will increase in learning. (Proverbs 9:9)

A wise man will hear and will increase learning; and a man of understanding shall attain unto wise counsels. (Proverbs 1:5)

As with most personality tests, you will identify with each classification. The one to focus on is the one that rings the MOST true for you. This is your primary archetype. You also have a secondary archetype. Dishonoring your archetypes will make you depressed, exhausted, or even ill because you're fighting with yourself. If you dress out of your archetype, you can be perceived as untrustworthy, dishonest, or devious because you're basically disguising your true self. Possibly even from yourself?

We're all born with innate manifestations of who we are. My second husband, Jeff, and I are opposite archetypes: Innovative and Loving. That could create thunder and lightning—or it could fill each other's voids. It depends if we're on our light or dark sides (which we all have). We come together on our secondaries because we are both "fun."

Our Source created us in a specific and deliberate way—not to create a miserable mystery of "who am I?" but to help us work together. My turning point put me on a path to discover and apply these truths. It helped me come to know and appreciate myself. It has been invaluable in my marriage and other relationships.

So who are you?

Istvan Zsako

Istvan Zsako is an entrepreneur, speaker, author, business consultant, and business strategist. Through learning to overcome the false identity, he has developed the victory mindset. He enjoys helping others find freedom, learn to see the abundant opportunities we all have and begin to live the life we have always desired.

· https://istvanzsako.com/

THE VICTORY MINDSET

Istvan Zsako

At the age of twenty-one, I thought life was going well. I had a job and made good money. I believed if I could be successful and make money, it would change everything. Unfortunately, all I found was disappointment and a busy schedule.

Growing up, my family struggled financially, and our home did not feel full of love. There were countless moments filled with yelling and anger that led to feelings of defeat, loneliness, failure, and a sense of worthlessness.

The feelings I had growing up became the person I was on the inside.

I identified myself as poor and destined to struggle. I let my past determine what my future had for me. I identified myself by the failures, troubled relationships, and bad decisions.

"This is who I am!" I told myself, "so this is what I will always get."

I avoided spending time by myself at all costs, instead hanging out in places with people I did not enjoy to keep myself from thinking about the things that happened to me.

My mind and soul were crying out for help. I wanted to be free of this pain, but I allowed it to continue to haunt me.

In the pursuit of happiness, I went looking for that inner peace through meditation, reiki, yoga, and other practices. I experienced moments of peace, but they were short-lived and temporary.

One day I decided to stop running from myself and spend time getting to know myself. Living with all the anger was wearing me out. I was tired of running and getting nowhere. I needed to understand what I was running from.

I stopped going to bars, clubs, parties, and social gatherings. I confined myself to my apartment and only left to work or get groceries. I did not take any calls from friends. I basically just disappeared. There was only one agenda: I needed to learn how to live with myself.

Sitting in my apartment all alone, I began to slip into a dark place filled with anger and resentment for the life I was living. I yelled out, "I did not ask for this life! Why did my parents have me if they were not going to love me?"

I was a sobbing mess, my eyes filled with tears; I felt hopeless and destined to carry this pain forever.

Memories flooded in of the times I cried myself to sleep after being hit or yelled at. I remembered all the times adults and teachers spoke hurtful words to me. They could have helped me, but they only saw me as a rebellious kid and pushed me away.

Most of my clothes were hand-me-downs from neighborhood friends. My parents didn't take care of me—they never even tried. I had grown to resent my parents for the childhood I lived.

In all my pain and anger, all I could see is what happened to "me." How they did this to "me." How they hurt "me." I was the victim of this not-so-great plan life had destined for me. I could not understand why this was happening to me.

"Haven't I suffered enough?"

Week after week, I revisited all the haunting memories I had been running from. I allowed myself to fully experience the feelings of having no self-worth. The many moments I wanted to end it all flooded into my mind.

In this dark place, I felt scared of what might happen. Would I end it all right here? I could not let myself continue to live the way I was living. In a moment of contemplating life or death, I asked myself, "How could someone do this to their own child?"

This is a question I had asked myself a thousand times before, but there was something different this time. Suddenly, I was reflecting on my parents as children. I remembered stories about my grandparents.

I began to imagine what my parents went through when they were growing up—the harsh discipline, abuse, fear, and emotional turmoil they must have gone through. The lack of a spiritual and emotional connection in my family started to become clear to me.

Have you ever heard the saying, "Hurt people hurt people?"

I became aware that my parents loved me out of their own understanding of love. In other words, they loved me the best they knew how. That was the limit to their ability to love others.

I began to experience an overwhelming feeling of empathy for my parents . . . and for myself.

Love is so much greater than what we can ever imagine. We think we know love, and then we get a glimpse of how much deeper love is. From that moment on,

I began to understand what love could be in my life. I decided to choose love; I decided to love myself.

At that point I became aware of the "false identity" I had accepted: a rebellious troublemaker who would never amount to anything, destined for broken relationships because I was unlovable. By accepting this false identity, I was the one keeping me from living the life I desired.

This awareness triggered a process inside of my heart and soul. I wanted to be angry, but somehow I could no longer feel the anger I used to feel toward my parents. Instead I chose to forgive them for hurting me. Reflecting on all of the times I had been hurt, I continued to forgive. Suddenly, I began to sense a freedom I had never experienced before. Those memories that used to take me to a dark place no longer had any control over me and how I felt.

I had experienced the true power of forgiveness.

By forgiving my parents, it never made what they did okay. Also, it did not make the pain magically disappear. But it allowed the beginning of the healing process to take place.

No longer was I blaming others for everything that went wrong in my life. The people that hurt me were not ruining my life. What happened to me was in the past; the pain I was carrying in the present is what was ruining my life.

I realized that the victim mentality had confined my mind and soul to places, persons, or events in my life. Hurtful things happened and that sucks, but I cannot change what happened. What I can do is to choose how I will respond to what happens in this life. Living in my past will only keep me from living in the present.

As I learned to break free of the painful memories and work toward overcoming these events, I was able to find freedom. In this freedom, I found the victory to overcome my past. I didn't know I was living my life as a victim until I found healing.

The process of forgiveness was the door to the healing I was longing for. I continued to reflect on all of the people that hurt me, spoke negative words to me, and pushed me away when I needed help. I wanted to be free of all the pain and hurt. This process took time, but through forgiveness, I methodically released all the old pain, hurt, and identity.

After I found healing, I was free to explore who I really am. What do I desire in life? What are my passions? What does the life I want look like? I was no longer stuck living my past and could start dreaming of the possibilities for my new life.

No longer do I focus on the life I hated, or the things I wish I could change. I focus on the life I desire to be living. Every day is a chance to learn something new, gain new experiences, and strive to be a better version of myself. I choose to focus on the solutions and take action. I no longer have problems in my business—only opportunities to make improvements for my clients and my staff. This has significantly changed how I live my life and run my business.

Through my experiences, I have adopted what I call the Victory Mindset. No longer am I a victim of what I experience. I cannot control or prevent everything that will happen to me, but I can change the outcome by choosing how I will respond to what happens. Best of all, I've developed the strength to help others along their journey, so they too can find their Victory Mindset.

CPSIA information can be obtained
at www.ICGtesting.com
Printed in the USA
LVHW051311300621
691545LV00016B/1345